50 Years At The Game

50 Years At The Game

A Sports Traveler's Journey

by John K. Moynahan

VANTAGE PRESS
New York

Typesetting by MAVERICK COMMUNICATIONS, Minneapolis, Minnesota.

FIRST EDITION

Published by Vantage Press, Inc.
516 West 34th Street, New York, New York 10001

Manufactured in the United States of America
ISBN: 0-533-12465-4

Library of Congress Catalog Card No.: 97-90732

0 9 8 7 6 5 4 3 2 1

Dedicated to the memory of John J. Moynahan (1910-1995), who took his five year old to Ebbets Field in 1946, the start of a wonderful sports journey that continues to this day. He is my sports idol; his wisdom, guidance, generosity and support made my sports journey, and anything else I accomplished in life, possible.

Contents & Illustrations

"Pittsburgh's here tomorrow Dad, let's come again"

With these words a five year old and his father left Ebbets Field in Brooklyn in July, 1946 after the boy's first baseball game. Dad and I didn't come back the next day, but I did come back to sports events, over three thousand times in the next half century; many fans go to more events, but few have experienced the VARIETY of events and venues that my fifty year journey has provided; my games have taken me to twenty seven states, five provinces and the District of Columbia, to 183 stadiums and arenas, most of them many times over; only about half the games have been in the areas where I lived at the time, the remainder were "road games"; I don't go to EVERY anything; I've gone to Super Bowls, World Series, the Stanley Cup Finals, but not every year; there is no favorite team that I follow passionately; several teams have been around as long as me, so I tend to favor those franchises over the newer ones, but my mood is never affected by who wins or loses. I don't cheer, boo, scream or carry on; I simply enjoy being at the game.

Many have said I should write a book about my memories, and views on how sports have changed, for better and worse, over the years; now that I've completed a full half century at the arenas and stadiums, it is time to write that book; I've chosen 250 days, covering only about ten per cent of the games I've attended; my reflections on these individual days capture what "50 Years at the Game" has meant to me.

My best memories are of days before luxury boxes pushed the most devout fans halfway to the sky, before public address announcers became cheerleaders and carnival barkers, before obnoxious music filled every otherwise silent moment, and before anthem singers who deserve a delay of game penalty. I enjoy and appreciate the games themselves, and only the games: football, hockey, baseball, basketball, even soccer. Although I've concentrated on pro events, I enjoy college sports as well; my favorite games are in the National Hockey League; a half century ago, hockey was confined to four large American cities; its following was limited to a handful of prep schools and hockey hotbeds such as Minnesota and Massachusetts; now the NHL is trying to mass market itself to Americans. Ironically, now that I live in supposed hockey country, Minnesota, I have to fly to Chicago, Toronto and San Jose to enjoy the NHL; but, I don't enjoy it as I did thirty years ago. As much as anything, the changing nature of my hockey journey mirrors dramatic changes in sport the last fifty years.

How can I recall with accuracy the date, time, location and other details of so many games over a half century? I've saved ticket stubs, scorecards, diary entries and other documents enabling me to verify my presence at each event; with data entered in the computer, it was simple to sort by location, sport, stadium, etc. so I'm confident of the accuracy of my recollections in this book. I don't expect complete agreement with all my views, but trust you'll enjoy sharing the 50 year sports journey. Let's get started.

50 Years At
The Game

Chapter I

The 40's

It Started In Brooklyn

It was Brooklyn's most glorious time. During the forties, New York City's largest borough would have been, by itself, America's third largest city; for a large city, the civic spirit and influence of Brooklyn was remarkable; perhaps it was because so many of those born there (such as myself) took part of that spirit wherever they moved. In the sixties, demographers calculated that 20% of the entire living United States population had been born in Brooklyn. The percentage is much lower today of course, both because many millions have since been born elsewhere and many of those native Brooklynites counted in the sixties study are (to quote a football commentator during a recent telecast) "dead at the present time".

Largely accountable for Brooklyn's civic spirit was the unifying influence of its beloved baseball team, the Brooklyn Dodgers. Even the present attachment of the city of Green Bay to its Super Bowl champion Packers pales in comparison to the identity forged between Brooklyn's citizens and its baseball team. I was born in Brooklyn during the winter season of 1940-41, when the New York Rangers were hockey's reigning Stanley Cup Champions (a fact that would become increasingly distressing to New Yorkers over the next fifty-four years as the Rangers repeatedly failed to capture the Cup again).

New York in the forties was a very sports conscious place. Everyone was defined as much by their answer to the question: "What are you, a Yankee, Giant or Dodger fan?" as by their occupation, religion or age. No one could avoid the question, plead indifference or have more than one answer; by definition, loyalty to one team implied disdain for the other two. My Uncle Bill grew up in Brooklyn and was an avid Dodger fan; my mother, whose family spoke their native Norwegian at home, and who probably couldn't name one Dodger player, did know that she was a native Brooklynite and declared herself a Dodger as well (albeit with far less passion than her brother). My father grew up in Manhattan, within walking distance of the Polo Grounds; his idols were the John McGraw era New York Giants; his allegiance never wavered; until he died in 1995 he wore with pride the orange and black cap with the Giants logo, his support for the team outliving their stay in New York by nearly four decades.

My own choice was easy; not to take sides, I declared myself a Yankee fan; of course at age four I wasn't quite sure what that meant; but when my uncle stayed with us for a while after his discharge from the Army, I would sit with him and listen to baseball on the radio; at first I was confused: I knew about radio and listened to the dramas, adventure and comedy shows of the World War II era; but where was this studio in which the audience was always purring, sometimes roaring, in the background; why did announcers slide cartons of cigarettes down a screen to a player who hit a home run? Gradually I came to understand that players did not come to the studio, but the station broadcast from the ballpark (and the hockey rink, boxing arena, basketball court and six-day bicycle race track).

For the rest of my childhood, I spent many hours listening to sports on the radio; one New York station, WMGM, was virtually an all sports station; not the inane babble that passes for sports talk today, they covered the GAMES, all of the games from the Garden, Army football, Dodgers baseball, Giants football, the Rangers, Knicks, college basketball, Rovers amateur hockey, track meets, boxing, tennis matches, whatever was going on.

As exciting as the mighty Yankees were, any New York baseball fan would have to have been equally interested in the National League, with its intense local Dodger-Giant rivalry; I followed the National League closely, but in the late forties became a Phillies fan; their team was on the rise, with great young stars who would eventually win the pennant in 1950; Phillies broadcasts boomed into Brooklyn as clearly as those of the New York teams; adopting the Phillies as my National League team of choice also kept me out of the Dodger-Giant rivalry. Now, a half century later, I have spring training tickets at two ball parks near my Gulf Coast condo, Jack Russell Stadium in Clearwater (the Phillies spring home) and Legends Field (the Yankees new ballpark in Tampa). The more things change, the more they stay the same.

Education was of the utmost importance in my home; public school was excellent; we learned arithmetic, reading and history; we memorized the Presidents of the United States in the order elected. Dad expanded the school curriculum and encouraged me to memorize the year by year participants in the World Series, and heavyweight champions from John L. Sullivan to Joe Louis. Soon, I was learning the roster of every major league team, and became intrigued by a list of cities appearing in the daily newspaper, sometimes in different sequence from the day before. Labelled "Standing of the Clubs", this simple newspaper box gave me lessons in reading and geography long before I ever saw a classroom.

I wondered where these places like Cincinnati and Chicago were, found them on maps, and learned what I could about the teams and their home towns; when I was nine I was on a local radio show called "Quiz Kids"; if one did well enough on the New York show, after a while you could be selected for the national program, broadcast from Chicago. When asked on the air why I would want to be on the Chicago program, I answered without hesitation "to see where the Cubs and White Sox play". I was an honest answer, but not good enough to get me to Chicago; I had to wait another 13 years for my first visit to Wrigley Field. But it was clear even then that I would be a sports traveler, and spend much of my life enjoying the spectacle and variety of the games I loved as a youth.

When my sports journey began, I was five years old and had not yet started school (nursery schools and kindergartens being virtually unknown in Brooklyn in the forties); but five years of life in Brooklyn was more than enough to prepare a boy for his first trip to the Dodgers' home, Ebbets Field.

GAME

Ebbets Field **1**

Chicago Cubs at Brooklyn Dodgers

While I'm sure Dad would have preferred a Giants game at the Polo Grounds, it was more convenient to take a five year old to Ebbets Field; we lived in the Midwood section, a half block from Brooklyn College and only a couple of miles from Ebbets Field. I remember little about this game; it took considerable research (in the absence of any surviving scorecard or ticket stub) to ascertain exactly which game in 1946 had been my first; Dad and I both remembered that the Dodgers had played the Cubs, but little else; since the Cubs played at Brooklyn eleven times a season, more data was needed to nail down the date; a few years before he died, Dad was recalling the baseball trips of my childhood, and in particular how spectators, after the game, were allowed to walk across the field and exit through the outfield fence. In Ebbets Field, this meant approaching the giant scoreboard along the right field wall and then using a door that led to Bedford Avenue. Dad remembered that as we approached the scoreboard leaving my first game, I looked at the scoreboard and exclaimed: "Pittsburgh here tomorrow, Dad, let's come again!" The 1946 National League schedule showed only one time the Pirates came to Ebbets Field the day after a Dodgers-Cubs afternoon game, so I had established exactly when my half century journey had begun.

Brooklyn, July 21, 1947

GAMES

Ebbets Field **2, 3**

Cincinnati Reds at Brooklyn Dodgers   (doubleheader)

To my father, sports meant baseball and, perhaps, boxing; football was of little interest to him; he, and most of his generation, disregarded hockey and basketball completely; by the time I was six, thanks to radio and newspapers, I had become an avid fan of all the sports but couldn't get my Dad interested enough to take me to anything except baseball; but each year he did take me at least once to each of New York City's three major league ballparks; this day must have been an ordeal for Dad the Giant fan sitting through a double-header as part of the largest Ebbets Field crowd of the season; we spent most of the afternoon sitting quietly in the upper deck above third base; the Dodger faithful were boisterous, my Dad and I quiet; we must have looked out of place to those around us, one of whom thought he had us figured out midway in the second game. Raising his voice, he looked at us and asked, in perfect Brooklynese: "Are youse from Cincinnati?" It must have seemed the only plausible explanation for our lack of exuberance.

6

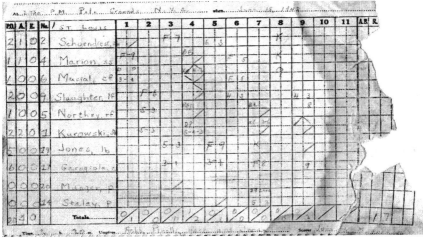

Polo Grounds

St. Louis Cardinals at New York Giants

The Polo Grounds was one of a kind; approaching the stadium from Eighth Avenue in upper Manhattan, one looked down on the roof of a horseshoe shaped park with short foul lines and 505 foot center field fence; the stadium was built into a hillside in upper Manhattan, just a few blocks from where my Dad spent his childhood. The Giants had a great history; overall, their franchise had been more consistently successful than the Dodgers but by the late forties the Giants had a limited following compared to the Yankees and Dodgers; unlike the other two New York teams who, between them made fourteen World Series appearances in the first ten years I followed baseball, the Giants were generally long on power, short on speed, limited in pitching and defense; good enough to be colorful and entertaining, but not often in serious contention for the pennant. Still, the Polo Grounds was my favorite of the three New York ball parks; on this day, I was most interested in Cardinal superstar Stan Musial, but he went hitless, twice hitting into double plays; three of my Dad's favorite Giants sluggers had big days; Sid Gordon went four for four with two home runs; John Mize and Willard Marshall both homered over the short right field fence as the Giants routed the Cardinals. Unknown to us at the time, during the sixth inning of the game, a thousand miles away in Wisconsin, the Pope family was welcoming their fourth child, baby Patty, into the world; many years later, that baby would get me in deep trouble at a sporting event, but that's getting nearly forty years ahead of the story.

At age 7, I carefully kept score of every play

GAME

Yankee Stadium **8**

Boston Red Sox at New York Yankees

A nother 1948 highlight was our annual Yankee Stadium visit; as an American League fan, it is not surprising that many of my favorite players: Ted Williams, the Di Maggio brothers, Joe of the Yankees and Dom of the Red Sox, Phil Rizzuto, and Yogi Berra among others, were on either the Yankees or the Red Sox. Ted Williams hit a home run in this game, but my most vivid memory is Joe DiMaggio playing center field as well as it can be played, killing a Red Sox rally with a great running catch. It was that memory of Joe D that was etched in my mind in the spring of 1996 when he stood, just a few feet away from me, to throw out the first ball at a Yankees spring training game.

New York,   September 16, 1949

GAME

Yankee Stadium **11**

Detroit Tigers at New York Yankees

T he 1949 season was nearly over before we made our annual Yankee Stadium visit; eventually, the 1949 pennant race went down to the final day before the Yankees outlasted the Red Sox to capture the pennant by one game; as the season entered its final two weeks every game was critical; since my father was unconvinced that television was here to stay, my contact with the Yankees had been strictly by radio and newspapers until the Tigers came in for a late season series; a fascinating 1949 Yankee was pitcher Tommy Byrne, a better than average left-hander and, most interestingly an excellent hitter often used to pinch hit by Yankee manager Casey Stengel; because New York City public schools had half day schedules, I went to grade school for either four morning or four afternoon hours daily; my fourth grade class had a morning schedule in the fall so I was able to go to the stadium if Dad took a Friday afternoon off. Tommy Byrne did not disappoint, pitching a complete game victory, and hitting a triple to deep center field, only to be thrown out trying for an inside the park home run. Dad nearly caught a souvenir foul ball for me, but it was snared away by a nearby spectator who removed his hat, used it as a glove, and went home with the official American League baseball. It would be thirty-six more years before I would catch a souvenir baseball.

Chapter II

The 50's

Starting The Journey

During the fifties I followed all sports very closely via radio, television and print media; I subscribed to The Sporting News, Sport Magazine, Sports Illustrated and every yearbook, magazine guide I could find; my attendance at pro sports would still be limited to major league baseball; as the decade ended I was a college sophomore; my parents were proud I was a history major, but perhaps distressed to know that much of my time in the library was spent researching the history of sports, reading every newspaper sports section of the preceding 30 years.

GAME

Shibe Park   15

Cleveland Indians at Philadelphia Athletics

I would have preferred my first game outside New York to be a Phillies game, but Dad chose the date for our Philadelphia trip and it was the Athletics playing at Shibe Park (later known as Connie Mack Stadium) that Saturday afternoon; we took the train to the North Philadelphia station, just a couple of blocks from the main rotunda entrance at 21st and Lehigh; the park looked like an enlarged Ebbets Field; we had a good view into the Athletics dugout where manager Connie Mack directed the team in street clothes, not a uniform; Mack owned the team and wore a business suit in the dugout; he never stepped on the field since he was not in uniform; strange as this practice may seem, Mack was not the first manager I'd seen in street clothes. Burt Shotton, the Dodger manager at this time, also did not wear a uniform. Very few tapes exist of game broadcasts from this era; remarkably, however, several years ago I did obtain a tape of the actual radio broadcast of this game, my journey's first of over two hundred stops in Philadelphia.

GAME

Roosevelt Hall Gym  17

Manhattan College at Brooklyn College

It was the golden age of college basketball in New York City, but Dad had no interest; I would have loved the great doubleheaders at the Garden, featuring national powerhouses NYU and CCNY; those two teams were devestated by the point shaving scandals of 1950, so whatever slight hope I might have had of going to the Garden for anything other than the circus was shattered; Dad came to believe that all of college basketball, a sport he cared little for to begin with, was corrupt. One player, Junius Kellogg of Manhattan College, got Dad's attention by refusing bribes and exposing some of those involved in fixing college games; this made Manhattan's team legitimate in Dad's mind, so he agreed to the half block walk to see them play; I next saw Manhattan basketball forty four years later, when they upset Oklahoma in the NCAA regionals at Memphis.

Brooklyn, July 4, 1951

GAMES

19, 20 Ebbets Field

(doubleheader) New York Giants at Brooklyn Dodgers

A s a boy, I never fully appreciated Dad's ability to come up with the best seats at New York sports events. Spending the Fourth of July in boxes behind the Dodger dugout was no small feat; an estimated thirty-five thousand would-be ticket buyers were turned away from Ebbets Field this day; somehow, we avoided the chaos and sat through twenty innings of what must have been agony for a Giant fan; the Dodgers swept the two games enroute to a 13 1/2 game lead over the second place Giants before the Giants September rally forced the famous three game National League pennant playoff.

Brooklyn, July 16, 1951

GAME

21 Ebbets Field

Cincinnati Reds at Brooklyn Dodgers

I enjoy baseball only when I am sitting somewhere between the bases, the lower the better; but even an upper deck seat in the infield suits me far better than any seat beyond the bases. Only once did I ever sit in the bleachers; school and playground groups were given free seats in the most remote parts of the ballpark. Newspaper accounts would show a paid attendance of say ten thousand but a total of fifteen thousand, the difference being the thousands of kids admitted free, but only to the bleachers. Just this once, I was among that crowd, with an excellent view of Duke Snider's back, but otherwise unable to appreciate the game, given my great distance from home plate and proximity to rowdy youngsters, few of whom cared as I did about the game itself.

GAMES

Fenway Park **22, 23**

Philadelphia Athletics at Boston Red Sox (doubleheader)

My family spent at least a month each summer on Cape Cod, where Dodger and Giant fans were scarce; the Red Sox and Yankees got most of the attention; a few contrarians liked the National League Boston Braves, but the Red Sox were far more popular. While the Cape is now quite accessible to New York and Boston, in those days the trip was arduous on overcrowded two lane highways; once settled in our summer home, we rarely went anywhere except the beach; afternoons were spent playing pick-up baseball, pretending to be Williams or DiMaggio, while placing a radio close enough to follow the action of the real Yankees and Red Sox. After several summers of trying, I convinced Dad to take me to Boston; a rainout delayed our trip a day, but made my first Fenway visit a doubleheader on a brutally hot August afternoon; we sat just above the first base dugout; my father, a National Leaguer was bored, and most of all, hot; in contrast I was riveted to the action; our seats looked squarely at the "Green Monster" left field wall; by the time we started the long drive back to the Cape, Fenway had become my favorite ballpark, and it remains my favorite to this day.

 ALL-TIME FAVORITE BASEBALL STADIUMS:

1. Fenway Park, Boston
2. Dodger Stadium, Los Angeles
3. Comiskey Park (old), Chicago
4. Tiger Stadium, Detroit
5. Wrigley Field, Chicago
6. Met Stadium, Minnesota
7. Polo Grounds, New York
8. 3Com Park, San Francisco

Queens, New York,   October 3, 1951

Every New Yorker of my generation remembers their exact whereabouts at two unforgettable moments, when JFK was assassinated in 1963 and when Bobby Thomson hit the "shot heard round the world" in 1951. The level of drama in the 1951 playoff is hard to imagine today; in a playoff for the pennant, the teams split two games, leaving a deciding game to be played at the Polo Grounds the afternoon of October 3. In this day of free agents moving from team to team, passionate rivalries of the fifties will never be duplicated; the Dodger-Giant rivalry was the most passionate of all; Dodger fans disliked Giant fans, players disliked players; some Giant fans never accepted Dodger manager Leo Durocher when he became Giants manager in 1948; Dodger great Jackie Robinson, when traded to the Giants near the end of his career, retired rather than don the uniform of the hated rival. Sal Maglie helped the Dodgers win a pennant in 1956, but in Brooklyn will best be remembered as an intimidating Giant pitcher, an antagonist in bitter bean-ball wars of the early 1950s. In this intense, emotional atmosphere the National League pennant was decided in the most dramatic fashion imaginable; Bobby Thomson hit Ralph Branca's 0-1 pitch into the lower of the deck in the ninth inning to turn a 4-2 Dodger lead into a 5-4, pennant winning, Giant victory. I was not at the game that afternoon; in fact only about thirty five thousand people were; ironically the demand for tickets for these two teams' fourth of July battle had been far greater. While I was not at the game, I was not in school either. Dad still didn't believe in television; however, I endeared myself to aunts and uncles who had no children but did, more importantly, have television. I watched the game at an apartment in Queens, close enough to Brooklyn to hear the moan of agony as Thomson's home run gave the Giants the pennant. The dramatic moment still is rebroadcast on television and radio more frequently than any other sporting event. Shortly after Thomson's unforgettable home run, Dad bought our first television and we spent much of the next several years watching baseball and boxing together; I managed to find time for lots of televised hockey and basketball as well; one black and white television was a luxury then; now I have a cluster of five screens in my living room, and multiple satellite receivers to bring every game, in every sport into the living room; in the last half century, I have watched at least a portion of many thousands of sports events on television. Still, the most dramatic single moment in any game I've watched came at the Polo Grounds before my family owned even one television.

GAME

Ebbets Field   **28**

St. Louis Cardinals at Brooklyn Dodgers

By 1952 my family had moved from Brooklyn to the suburbs, a world away from Ebbets Field; the Dodgers lasted five more years in Brooklyn, but this was my last trip to the aging ballpark. The spirit and identity of Brooklyn left when the Dodgers moved to Los Angeles for the 1958 season; yet, what the Dodgers did is just what millions of their fans did, move out of Brooklyn; those who romanticize the Brooklyn Dodgers and Ebbets Field have certainly not been on Bedford Avenue lately, nor have they been to Dodger Stadium, still the most beautiful in all of baseball. Just like their fans, when the neighborhood deteriorated, the Dodgers moved to a better one; by the time the Dodgers left for Los Angeles, I was sixteen, living in the suburbs and was no more likely to set foot in Ebbets Field than in Los Angeles. In many locales, teams are taken for granted, with the importance of pro sports to the fabric and spirit of a community vastly underestimated; in retrospect, whatever incentive was needed for the Dodgers to stay in Brooklyn (or to use a more recent example, the Browns in Cleveland) would have been worth it. If a community is major league, it must offer a major league facility or one will be found elsewhere. Brooklynites, sadly, learned the hard way.

Washington, August 23, 1952

GAME

Griffith Stadium **29**

Detroit Tigers at Washington Senators

What more educational experience could an eleven year old have than to visit the Nation's Capital in the heat of a Presidential campaign. General Eisenhower, campaigning to end two decades of Democratic administrations, promised to "clean up the mess in Washington". Dad and I took the train from New York early Saturday; the only mess we saw in Washington was muddy streets caused by a summer of heavy rains; my most memorable, and educational excursion was to Griffith Stadium on a hot, humid Saturday night. From the outside, it looked like a somewhat non-descript old ballpark, vaguely similar to Ebbets Field; looking at the huge playing area, it more resembled Yankee Stadium; over the years, both Dad and I visited Washington frequently, but never again together; eventually I became familiar with all the historic sites, but my first visit concentrated on baseball and the famous Washington Senators: First in War, First in Peace and Last in the American League. By the next time I saw this team play, they had become the Minnesota Twins.

New York,   July 7, 1953

GAMES

31, 32   Polo Grounds

(doubleheader)   **Philadelphia Phillies**
at New York Giants

I couldn't get enough baseball, and was always on the lookout for doubleheaders; when an early season rainout set up a twi-nighter at the Polo Grounds with the Phillies I urged Dad to get tickets; my rationale was to celebrate my successful completion of seventh grade, not that my mastery of the seventh grade curriculum was ever in much doubt; Dad got the tickets, and the last laugh; his Giants swept my Phillies in both ends of the doubleheader.

New York,   August 7, 1954

GAME

34   Polo Grounds

Milwaukee Braves at New York Giants

The tradition of "Ladies Day" at major league ballparks originally meant that a man purchasing a game ticket could bring any woman to the game free of charge; implicit in the concept of Ladies Day were some politically incorrect notions, principally that females, without the aid of a male would be disinterested or unable to attend baseball games; these notions captured the role of many women in the fifties, and were certainly descriptive of my own household. So, for a total cost of about five dollars, two paid tickets for my Dad and myself, the entire family could spend Saturday afternoon at the Polo Grounds; the Giants were on their way to their most successful season ever; Dad and I loved the games, although the "Ladies" of our Ladies Days, my mother and sister, would have probably opted for Jones Beach given any voice in the matter.

New York, April 15, 1955

GAME

Polo Grounds **36**

Brooklyn Dodgers at New York Giants

Good Friday 1955 is a landmark in my sports journey for three reasons: it was the first game I attended without adult supervision; two friends and I took the train and subway to the Polo Grounds, bought ourselves box seats, and got back on the subway after the game; secondly, it is the earliest game from which I still possess the ticket stub, no doubt because it was the first ticket I ever had to purchase; thirdly, this would be the last time I would ever see either the NEW YORK Giants or BROOKLYN Dodgers; the two teams remained in New York through the 1957 season, but Long Island high schoolers could find plenty to do without venturing into the urban wastelands surrounding New York's National League ballparks.

New York, August 12, 1956

GAMES

Yankee Stadium **39, 40**

Baltimore Orioles at N Y Yankees (doubleheader)

Whenever I went to Yankee Stadium as a teenager, I would sneak into the first row of mezzanine seats behind home plate, directly behind the press box; one specific seat always seemed to be vacant; don't look for it now, as the owner's luxury box occupies this whole section of the original Stadium. Remarkably no one ever challenged my occupancy of what Dad called "your seat at Yankee Stadium". Dad sat wherever he was supposed to, since he was reluctant to risk being caught sneaking into the best seats in the house; this day I spent eighteen innings without taking my eyes off the field, less because of concentration on the game than fear of turning my head and catching the eye of an unfriendly usher.

New York,　May 2, 1958
GAME
41 Yankee Stadium
Kansas City Athletics at New York Yankees

It was my senior year in high school, and the first baseball season in which New York was an American League city, the Giants and the Dodgers now resident on the West Coast; Dodger fans were in mourning, a depression which affects some Brooklynites to this day; the Giants had been fading for several years and their loss had less impact. Even my Dad the Giant fan quickly shifted his attention (if not his complete partisanship) to the Yankees. I had long since stopped going to Giant or Dodger games, so my concern was the amount of baseball on television; in fact, there was more than ever; most Yankee road games were televised, Channel 9 picked up a full schedule of Phillies games and another station showed several dozen National League games featuring the Dodgers and Giants as visiting teams, so my life was unaffected by the demise of New York's great historic National League rivalry. My one game in the 1958 season resulted from being given four box seats (and the afternoon off) by my high school principal; together with three other students we drove to the Stadium; even though we had good seats, I spent a few innings back at my "favorite seat" in the mezzanine first row, for old times sake.

Hartford,　September 27, 1958
GAME
42 Jessee Field
Williams College at Trinity College

Off campus for the first time in my ten day college career (save for nightly beer runs to Cal King's Package Store), I spent a miserable rainy afternoon watching my college lose to.Trinity. Would all four years be this miserable? Hardly. Williams had very competitive teams for the most part; and this trip got better once the game ended and the parties began; the following season, I began covering football and basketball on the radio, financing my travel to fraternity parties at such unlikely spots as Waterville, Maine and Evansville, Indiana.

Chapter III

The 60's

Traveling On My Own

As the sixties began, I was a sophomore at Williams College; I had still never been on an airplane. My sports travel had expanded to include college games throughout New England, but I had yet to attend my first professional football, basketball or hockey game. By the end of the decade, I would have an MBA degree, a nine month pregnant wife, and five years experience in the management consulting business; I moved from New York to Philadelphia to San Francisco and back to New York; my sports journey had begun in earnest, and I was a regular at NFL and AFL pro football, as well as NHL and NBA games, adding 453 events to my total during the decade.

Despite the regularity of Yankee and Dodger participation, I had never attended a World Series game; suddenly, the opportunity arose; one member of my fraternity was the son of a part-owner of the National League Champion Pittsburgh Pirates. Anyone who wanted to drive to Pittsburgh or New York could attend the games as guests of the Pirates. Several of my friends jumped at the opportunity and as a result were at Forbes Field for the second (to Bobby Thomson) most dramatic home run in baseball history, Bill Mazeroski's 1960 Series winner, and the subsequent celebrations throughout the city of Pittsburgh. No one was a greater sports fan than I was, but I turned down the invitation, for a foolish reason; as a Yankee partisan and American League fan, I felt it would be hypocritical to accept the hospitality of the Pirates. How silly of me. Of course I told my parents I turned down the opportunity because I had to study, an even more far-fetched explanation. It would be thirteen more years before I got to a World Series, and when I did I had to pay my own way.

Boston, April 18, 1961
GAME

Fenway Park **96**

Minnesota Twins at Boston Red Sox

Back at Fenway for the first time in ten years, I saw the new Minnesota Twins (who, until this season, had been the Washington Senators); the Twins had not yet played a game in Minnesota. The expansion of Met Stadium was being completed, so the Twins started their first season with a nine game Eastern road trip. Two things stand out about this game, the cold and the crowd. The announced crowd was in the two thousand range, which is probably a more accurate count of the number of numbed individual hands and feet present; I've never been colder at any event, not even football in Chicago in January; the game still had great interest for me; the Twins (and the first new baseball teams in my lifetime, the 1961 expansion Senators and Angels) were the only major league franchises I had never seen play. Little did I suspect that one day, nearly thirty years later, my own relocation would make these Minnesota Twins my own home team.

New York,   December 6, 1961

GAME

107   Madison Square Garden

Chicago Blackhawks
at New York Rangers

Being a hockey fan in New York in my youth meant being a Rangers fan. It was difficult enough to follow the Rangers, impossible to get enough information about the other five teams to become a fan of, say, the Toronto Maple Leafs. Most New Yorkers knew little of hockey, but those who did were passionate Rangers fans. My first NHL game was well worth the eight hour round trip drive to Manhattan with college friends; the Hawks and Rangers played quickly, and with intensity; there were no commercial time outs, no delays for video review, and the intermissions took only twelve minutes; while the Zamboni ice cleaning machine had been invented, this arena had not yet acquired one, so the ice resurfacing was done by maintenance workers dragging barrels of dripping water from one end of the Garden ice to the other; the Blackhawks, defending Stanley Cup Champions, beat the Rangers this night; you truly had to be there; the game was not broadcast on radio or television in either New York or Chicago; only the seven thousand or so in the building could follow the game as it happened; and it happened quickly, with few stoppages in play; by nine thirty we were headed back to Williamstown; it was well worth it; I definitely got my three dollars worth.

Amherst, Mass.,   March 2, 1962

GAME

120   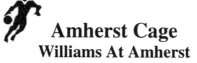 Orr Rink

Williams at Amherst

GAME

121   Amherst Cage

Williams At Amherst

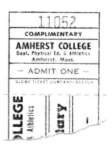

It seemed so important for four years, particularly the rivalries with Amherst and Wesleyan; even though the games drew sparse crowds in small on-campus gyms, stadiums and, worst of all, outdoor hockey rinks, Williams-Amherst took on an imagined importance equivalent to Yankees-Red Sox or Knicks-Celtics; Williams was generally more competitive, going as far as the NCAA small college basketball finals in 1961; but an Amherst game was always important because of the closely linked history of the two schools; these games signalled the end of the winter season, as there was no post-season play in the offing for Williams this year; Williams posted impressive victories in both sports, and our victory parties continued far into the night; in all the jubilation, I was unaware of the dramatic change about to take place in my sports priorities; in the thirty five seasons since this day at Amherst, I have attended only three college hockey games; and, it would be over thirty two years before I would next attend a college basketball game.

GAME

Boston Garden 124

New York Rangers at Boston Bruins

There is (or at least was) no such thing as a casual hockey fan; those, like myself, who followed the sport with a passion when only six teams were in the league, put NHL hockey on a level above all other sports. I'm a dedicated, knowledgeable fan of the other three major team sports, but nothing takes precedence over my love of the NHL; and for thirty four seasons, starting this night and ending at the last ever Stanley Cup game in the building, a frequent stop on my hockey schedule was the intimate, rowdy Boston Garden; the Bruins were mediocre in 1962, but this was nevertheless a vitally important game; the Rangers, who rarely qualified for the playoffs were battling Detroit for the final playoff berth; they needed a win at Boston and got it; I headed for spring break with great optimism that my next NHL game would be my first Stanley Cup playoff game.

New York, April 3, 1962

GAME

Madison Square Garden 125

Toronto Maple Leafs at New York Rangers

In my first fifteen years following the Rangers, they made the playoffs only four times and had played only eight post season games at the Garden. The annual circus visit had priority at the Garden, so sometimes "home" playoff games would be moved to Toronto or Boston, a practice which would be beyond unthinkable for any NHL team today; but the 1962 Rangers made the playoffs, and worked around the circus schedule to play home games at the Garden. I had spent spring break in the Bahamas (my first airplane trip, and, amazingly, not for sports) and returned to find the Rangers trailing Toronto two games to one; my Dad was not a hockey fan, but this was one of those infrequent times when hockey took center stage in New York. The Garden was the place to be; knowing how much I would want to be there, my Dad had two side loge seats, the best in the house, for game four waiting for me when I arrived home. I don't think I've ever received a more appreciated gift. The Rangers won to tie the series, but lost the next two at Toronto to end their Cup hopes; there would be another five year hiatus between Ranger playoff games at the Garden.

Springfield, Mass., April 21, 1962

GAME

126  Eastern States Coliseum

Buffalo Bisons at Springfield Indians

With only six teams in the NHL, many world class players could not crack a major league roster. Many of these players were with the Springfield Indians, owned by Hall of Famer Eddie Shore who ruled with an iron hand and closed checkbook; his team was independent, meaning his players could move to the NHL only by making a trade with Shore; as a result, it was commonly believed that the Indians may have been equal in talent to some NHL teams, and were, at worst, the seventh best team in pro hockey. Their home was the ancient (even then) "Big E" on the exposition grounds in West Springfield; only an hour or so from the campus, Indians games were a reasonable alternative to longer trips to Boston or New York. The 1962 Calder Cup finals matched the Indians with the Buffalo Bisons, a team memorable mostly for their uniform logo, a Pepsi-Cola bottle cap image with the word Buffalo spelled out where it would normally read "Pepsi".

New York, August 20, 1962

GAMES

127, 128 Polo Grounds

(doubleheader) Pittsburgh Pirates at New York Mets

The National League returned, sort of, to New York in 1962 with the most inept team in baseball history, the "Amazin'" Mets. Embraced by fans still stung by the departure of the Dodgers and Giants, the Mets played at the Polo Grounds; unlike Ebbets Field which was demolished to make way for a housing project, the Polo Grounds was still standing and had been used for football, soccer, boxing and even a rodeo since the Giants left for San Francisco. In Flushing Meadow Queens a new stadium was taking shape, but for this forgettable 120 defeat season, the Polo Grounds was home to the Mets; my one visit was a twi-night doubleheader; predictably, the Pirates won both games; the Mets played one more year at the Polo Grounds, but this was my last ever visit to my favorite of the original three New York City major league ballparks.

New York,   October 28, 1962

GAME

Yankee Stadium 134

Washington Redskins At New York Giants

GAME

Madison Square Garden 135

Chicago Blackhawks at New York Rangers

The Giants owned New York in the sixties; after their NFL championship games of 1958 and 1959 (both of which they lost), and fortified by the perfect marriage of the National Football League and CBS television, the Giants were the hottest ticket in town. Sunday afternoons, everybody who was anybody (and many, like myself, wo were nobody) was at Yankee Stadium; thousands more headed toward Connecticut motels to see the sold out, blacked out home games on television. My father had access to the best seats for all New York sports events; rarely did he go to football games himself, but I never had trouble finding a companion for a Giant game; at my first NFL game, I saw quarterback put on a show unmatched by anything since. Y. A. Tittle connected for a record seven touchdown passes in a single game. Following the Giant game, which normally ended about 5pm, my routine was to head to midtown, catch a bite to eat and settle into my seat at the Garden by the time the puck was dropped promptly at 7pm to start the Rangers game.

GAMES ATTENDED: *(through 5/19/97)*

Professional Hockey 1811
Pro Baseball 705
Pro Football 299
Pro Basketball 194
College Basketball 93
College Football 41
Pro Soccer (outdoor) 16
Pro Soccer (indoor) 11
College Hockey 9
Olympic Soccer 1

TOTAL: **3,180**

Princeton, Nov. 24, 1962

GAME
140  Palmer Stadium

Dartmouth at Princeton

ollege and prep school students had long congregated in New York over Thanksgiving break to network, party, and meet members of the opposite sex; five months after graduation these festivities were still much to my liking; with two friends and three college women, I headed for the Princeton campus; one of our group was a Princeton alum, so we were able take part in all aspects of a college football weekend including, almost incidentally, the game. Out of college, and into both the workplace and graduate school, returning to campus, any campus, was a welcome reminder of a wonderful part of my life which had ended with graduation. This particular campus and stadium reminded me of my childhood, when Ivy League football was very serious business; by 1962, big time college football had moved out of the East, certainly out of the Ivy League, but watching the Big Green take on the Princeton Tiger brought back memories of football on the radio at a time when Princeton and Dartmouth, as well as Penn, Cornell and the other Ivies, played as high profile games as Notre Dame, Texas, Michigan, and Alabama.

New York,   December 27, 1962

GAME
144 Madison Square Garden

Boston Bruins at New York Rangers

uring the 1996 Stanley Cup playoffs a puck sailed into the Pittsburgh bench and clipped coach Ed Johnston on the forehead; he went out for stitches and returned in a few minutes; I immediately recalled this 1962 game when Johnston played goal for the Bruins; his team was taking a pounding from the Rangers, and, to add injury to insult a Ranger shot caught Johnston square in the face; the game was delayed while Johnston was stitched and his blood scraped from the ice. In 1962, teams had only one goaltender on the roster; most goalies did not wear a mask, and only one or two players in the whole league wore helmets. In retrospect, that seems reckless and dangerous; but the game has changed in more ways than just the added protective equipment; the sixties player had respect for the opponent, kept his stick (and shot) down, and dared not run an opponent from behind. The game did a far better job of policing itself three decades ago than it does today.

GAMES

Wrigley Field  156, 157

St. Louis Cardinals   (doubleheader)
at Chicago Cubs

Always fascinated by the varying characteristics of sports stadia and their surrounding communities, I was now able to explore these venues on my own; heading for Iowa to visit a girlfriend, I circled Forbes Field in Pittsburgh several times; the Pirates were on the road but I wanted to at least see the stadium from the outside; the next day I did the same at Comiskey Park and then went to Wrigley Field for my first Chicago sports events; Chicago has since become my favorite sports city, but it was a little uncomfortable on this steamy Sunday afternoon with Wrigley Field jammed way beyond capacity by Cubs fans and a large contingent of Cardinal zealots; the stadium and the fans reminded me of the passionate inhabitants of Ebbets Field; Wrigley Field, with its contours matched to the surrounding city blocks sits in a neighborhood that remains attractive and liveable; it is today's closest approximation of what Ebbets Field and its surroundings were like in my childhood.

St. Louis, August 4, 1963
GAMES

Busch Stadium 158, 159

Philadelphia Phillies   (doubleheader)
at St. Louis Cardinals

My week in Iowa ended at 4am Sunday, as I needed seven hours to drive to another Sunday doubleheader, this time in St. Louis. By the time I got to St. Louis I was ready to park at the first space available. A block from the Stadium, people were parking cars in their driveways and backyards; I chose one, made a mental picture of the house and settled into a box seat for a long afternoon of baseball. Six hours later I had seen the Cardinals lose for the fourth time on two consecutive Sundays and went to my car to start a two day drive back to New York. Only then did I discover that on all four sides of old Busch Stadium in northeast St. Louis, all homes look exactly alike; I knew my car was no more than a block from the stadium, but in which direction? Ultimately, with the baseball crowd gone and darkness approaching, I hailed a taxi and had it drive me block by block until we were flagged down by a resident looking for the owner of the one car still parked in his backyard. I paid the taxi, got in my car and had a safe trip home; I've had many great times in St. Louis since, and even went to old Busch Stadium once more before it was abandoned in 1968, but my first St. Louis memory will always be those "extra innings" searching for my car.

New York, November 17, 1963

GAME

172  Yankee Stadium

San Francisco 49ers at New York Giants

GAME

173 Madison Square Garden

Toronto Maple Leafs at New York Rangers

Look at pictures of sports events from the sixties and observe the crowd in the background; Yankee Stadium (and even the Garden) crowds were upwards of ninety percent male, most dressed in suits, topcoats and hats. Attending the Giants game was an extension of the work week; tickets were consumed by corporations and Wall Street firms, and much deal-making was done while Y.A. Tittle was looking for an open receiver. There were a few zealots in the crowds, such as the man in the leopard-skin coat who serenaded the crowd on his trombone from ice level before all Rangers games, but crazies were the exception not the rule. Those of us whose parents regularly got us the corporate seats dressed with respect, and acted civil. A behavioral indiscretion could jeopardize the continued availability of tickets for these Sunday sports doubleheaders. Unknown to anyone on this Sunday, however, was that before another Giants-Rangers Sunday would arrive, everyone's lives would be touched by the most shocking event of our lifetime.

FOOTBALL GAME SUMMARY: (through 1996 season)

		Most Frequent Home Teams	
NFL reg. season	224		
NFL post season	24		
AFL reg. season	15	Minnesota Vikings	79
Super Bowl	7	New York Jets	43
Pro Bowl	5	New York Giants	41
NFL pre-season	20	Tampa Bay Buccaneers	29
USFL reg. season	4	San Francisco 49ers	16

TOTAL: 299

Everyone can remember their exact whereabouts on that tragic Friday afternoon when President Kennedy was assassinated. I was working on the trading desk of a Wall Street firm; fast reaction to news and rumors was the lifeblood of trading; but once this news report was confirmed as truth not rumor, hundreds of normally blinking phone lights shut off as abruptly as in a power outage. All America was stunned; after an hour or so, people silently drifted their separate ways; until this day, political assassinations happened in the third world, or in history books; the first of far too many had shattered the spirit of America; two hours after the President died, I was on a commuter train to my parents home in Long Island, ironically departing the train at the station where, 30 years later, a berserk madman gunned down innocent commuters. A new, violent America was a reality.

Springfield, November 23, 1963

GAME

Eastern States Coliseum 175

Cleveland Barons at Springfield Indians

Virtually everything, sports and otherwise, was postponed or cancelled for the weekend of mourning; surprisingly, in the slain President's home state of Massachusetts, a pro hockey game was played on Saturday night; after postponing their Friday home game, the seventh best team in hockey took the ice at 8pm Saturday evening, while most of America was still mourning and television and radio was airing continuous news updates and serene music. I believe the rationale for playing the game had to do with the fact that, in 1963, nearly every player in both the NHL and the minor pro leagues was a Canadian, not American citizen; in no way were the hockey teams ignoring or minimizing the tragedy, but the decision to play after only one day of cancellations illustrates how hockey was at that time a completely Canadian game, which happened to play its games in a number of American cities. Still, I was amazed the game was played, but glad I was there; contemplating the terrible tragedy and its implications would be something we Americans could do for the rest of our lives. We wouldn't have to cancel any more games in order to do so.

New York, November 24, 1963

GAME

176  Yankee Stadium

St. Louis Cardinals at New York Giants

GAME

177 Madison Square Garden

Toronto Maple Leafs at New York Rangers

I t was the same, yet so different; the Giants in the afternoon, the Rangers at night. Pete Rozelle later regretted allowing games to be played, calling it his greatest mistake as NFL commissioner; the rival American Football League postponed its schedule; the NFL games were not on television or radio, but they were played, and I'm glad they were; driving to the Stadium Sunday morning the news came that Lee Oswald had been shot by Jack Ruby in the Dallas police station; the situation was becoming increasingly bizzare. To say that the Stadium crowd was distracted would be a huge understatement. The Cardinals and Giants played with a predictable lack of intensity; the crowd, a full house as usual, was subdued and silent; for my part, I would rather be at a game than anywhere else but it was difficult to concentrate on the action on the field; the Garden that night was closer to normal; it was easier to escape reality in the hockey environment, for some reason.

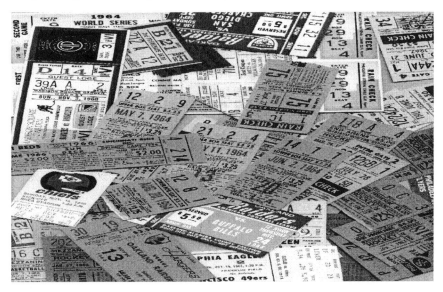

GAME

Connie Mack Stadium **184**

Pittsburgh Pirates at Philadelphia Phillies

I served six months at Fort Dix New Jersey in 1964 and learned the value of a low profile; never volunteer, always look busy, and when allowed off the base, get off and don't come back until late at night. These "reservists rules to live by" combined with the proximity of Philadelphia enabled me to spend much of the Phillies most memorable (and ultimately, most disappointing) season at Connie Mack Stadium. The Phillies observed the military equivalent of Ladies Day, offering free admission to soldiers in uniform. The economic appeal notwithstanding, there was no way I wanted to be in uniform more than necessary; I bought tickets, dressed as I liked, and slipped back into Fort Dix as late and as unobtrusively as possible. This night the drive back was memorable, as I listened on radio to one of the most dramatic Stanley Cup Finals games of all time, in which Bob Baun, playing on an injured leg later found to be broken, scored an overtime goal to force a seventh game and set the stage for the Leafs third consecutive Stanley Cup.

New York,   June 25, 1964

GAME

Shea Stadium **190**

Pittsburgh Pirates at New York Mets

While I was at Fort Dix, Flushing Meadows came alive with the 1964 World's Fair and, alongside, the multi-tiered new home of the Mets, Shea Stadium. Eventually I did go to the Fair, but my first priority was to go to the new ballpark; within a few years Shea was rundown, dirty and crowded, but on this sunny afternoon before a sparse crowd, it was perfect. When I returned to my parents' home after the game, I learned I had received an excellent job offer from a management consulting firm; I could hardly imagine that I would work there for over twenty-six years, make a good living, travel throughout the world and, by planning trips carefully, visit virtually every major stadium and arena in North America.

Los Angeles, July 9, 1964

GAME

191 Chavez Ravine

Chicago White Sox at Los Angeles Angels

As far as I know, it was the only stadium with an alias; to all the world it was, and still is, known as Dodger Stadium, the world's most perfect ballpark. For a couple of years, the Angels also used the stadium, and called it Chavez Ravine (referring to the area of Los Angeles in which Dodger Stadium sits) for Angels home games. This was my first sporting event in California; the Angels were in only their fourth year of play, but had developed some fascinating players, and the beginning of a most interesting, often bizzare, sometimes tragic, history. What the Angels did not have (and, I would argue, to this day have not acquired) were fans. They had spectators, to be sure, but they did not have FANatics who paint their faces, dress head to toe in team colors and rampage through the team hotel on road trips. The Angels, for all their success and achievement, still have no fans; think about it; who has not known some zealot whose whole life was defined by a passion for the Cubs, or Celtics, or Duke Blue Devils? But has anyone ever known an Angels fan? Has any area ever had the National Guard on alert to deal with the influx of crazies traveling to Angels road games? Never. I've posed the same question hundreds of times, even inside Anaheim Stadium. No one yet has ever known an Angels fan.

New York,   September 12, 1964

GAME

202 Shea Stadium

Denver Broncos at New York Jets

The American Football League New York Titans changed their name to the Jets and moved from the Polo Grounds to Shea Stadium. Immediately, they gained an identity and a following. Once in Shea, the Jets absorbed enough of the thousands of football fans who couldn't get Giants tickets to assure capacity crowds; my friends in the Jet Pack don't always like to admit it, but Jet fans are direct descendants of Giant fans. My Dad's connections were as useful at Shea as at the Stadium; front row mezzanine box seats, plus for cold weather, a choice table in the Diamond Club, were mine for the asking; the only problem was that one had to get to the Stadium to enjoy these perks. The first Jets home game was a traffic fiasco; Saturday night at the Fair could back up traffic for miles by itself; add sixty thousand fans driving to the Jet game and disaster happened; fortunately, I left early for the game; as a result I arrived at Shea in the THIRD quarter; others were not so fortunate.

GAME

Franklin Field **203**

San Francisco 49ers at Philadelphia Eagles

Philadelphia sports fans are brutally critical, unforgiving and generally harder on local athletes than any other. They are equally intolerant of coaches and owners; the Eagles had given the city one of its rare championships in 1960 but performed erratically thereafter; owner Jerry Wolman signed Joe Kuharich to a lucrative contract as coach and traded away future Hall of Fame quarterback Sonny Jurgensen; the fans rebelled at a rebuilding plan for a team that, to the Eagle faithful, needed motivation for immediate success, not rebuilding. An opening game victory over the Giants bought Kuharich a week, but as the Eagles lost at home to the 49ers, the chant began: "Joe Must Go! Joe Must Go!"; and it didn't stop; Joe Must Go was the unifying slogan for frustrated Eagle fans for years (even after Joe did go).

GAME

Connie Mack Stadium **204**

Cincinnati Reds at Philadelphia Phillies

The Phillies put it all together in 1964; Gene Mauch, the charismatic strategist, was making all the right moves, until September. Jim Bunning, Chris Short and Art Mahaffey led a deep pitching staff. Richie Allen's powerful bat added further muscle to an already strong offense. The Phillies held first place most of the season and still had a safe lead going into the final two weeks; the next seven games would be at home, three with Cincinnati and four with Milwaukee; the pennant was within reach, World Series tickets had been sold, the pennant was the Phillies to lose; they could only beat themselves, which of course they did; in the biggest collapse in memory, night after night the Phillies found a different way to lose; the most bizarre came on this night during a scoreless game. Frank Robinson, one of the most fearsome hitters in baseball is at the plate with Chico Ruiz on third base. Ruiz, for reasons that defy explanation, takes off on the pitch and tries a steal of home. Who, in a thousand years of baseball would try a steal of home with the league's best hitter at the plate; had Robinson swung and hit a liner toward third, Ruiz might have been decapitated; but Robinson didn't swing, Ruiz who missed the sign was safe at home and the Phillies were beaten 1-0 beginning a string of ten consecutive losses and a blown pennant. It will be remembered as the darkest week in Philadelphia sports history, with its darkest moment occurring as Chico Ruiz stole home.

New York, Dec. 6, 1964

GAME

216  Yankee Stadium

Minnesota Vikings at New York Giants

G iant football at Yankee Stadium had been THE thing to do for years; but a two win, ten loss 1964 record helped me become aware of the brutal cold and wind in the open stands and the rapidly deterioriating surrounding area of the Bronx; in contrast, the tables by the window in the warm Diamond Club were only fifteen minutes from home, and the Jets were a team on the rise, committed to being successful on the field. Despite growing up with pro football in New York, I was never a passionate Giants fan so there was no strong allegiance to switch; Shea was just more convenient and comfortable; by the next year, when Joe Namath joined the Jets I became much more selective about accepting Giants tickets, but never missed a chance to go to a Jets game at Shea.

New York, May 26, 1965

GAME

241 Shea Stadium

Chicago Cubs at New York Mets

G oing to Shea for baseball was another matter altogether. The early Mets encouraged irrational fan behavior, presumably to distract attention from the team's irrational behavior on the field; fans were known for bringing banners to hang everywhere, and carrying on noisily regardless of the game action. But by 1965 the team itself was worth watching, just four years away from winning a World Series; only minutes from home, Mets games should be perfect summer entertainment; my friends and I tried, but unruliness was everywhere; who wants to be seated near the school band that brought their instruments (and extra drums) to the game, or near barbarians consuming beer at a pace such that by the time the eighth member is served, the first is ready for a refill; the beer vendor might as well have been kidnapped. Within a few years, Shea Stadium was much better; as the team improved, the clientele became correspondingly more knowledgeable and interested in the game; but in 1965, Mets baseball was an ordeal.

GAME
Madison Square Garden 256

Chicago Blackhawks at New York Rangers

Jim Brennan was a business associate and sports fan. He knew little about hockey, but watched the Rangers on television and thought he would enjoy going to a game. He had one irrational concern, however; on television, he had seen pucks fly into the crowd and worried that he would be hit with one; in fact, he cancelled the first couple of times we planned to go, but finally got up his courage to join me this Wednesday night at the Garden. (In retrospect, it would have been good had he also had the courage to tell his wife he was going to a hockey game, not that he would be working late at the office). My seats at the old Garden were three rows off the ice, just above the protective glass, inside the blue line to the right of the players' benches. When we got to the seats, Jim panicked; he had no idea we would be so close to the action; he was sure a puck would hit him. I reminded him that the goals were to our left and right, and no player's shot was so inaccurate that it would clear the side boards near center ice; I offered one hypothetical scenario; if the team to our left were penalized, conceivably one of their players might scale the puck in our direction to relieve the pressure from the onrushing power play. Strictly hypothetical, for eleven seconds. Then Moose Vasko of the Hawks is called for holding; Rangers, moving right to left, dump the puck into the Hawks zone. Bill "Red" Hay of the Hawks gathers in the puck at his own blue line and the rest is history; Hay lifts the puck over the glass, off Jim Brennan's skull, onward ten rows back into the arena. The game is twenty-nine seconds old; Ranger team physician Dr. Yanagazawa, better known for spinal fusions, stitched Jim's forehead and sent him back to our seats to ponder his post game press conference at home.

HOCKEY GAME SUMMARY: *(through 1996-97 season)*

NHL reg. season 1541
Stanley Cup Playoffs................ 187
NHL pre season 35
World Hockey Assn. 12
International Games 4
NHL All Star 3
Minor Pro Leagues........................ 29

TOTAL: 1,811

Most Frequent Home Teams	Regular Season Games	Stanley Cup Playoffs
New York Rangers	375	42
New York Islanders	218	24
Chicago Blackhawks	147	31
Minnesota North Stars	181	22
Philadelphia Flyers	148	20
Boston Bruins	65	16

New York,   November 28, 1965

GAME

259  Yankee Stadium

Chicago Bears at New York Giants

GAME

260 Madison Square Garden

Toronto Maple Leafs at New York Rangers

Ten days later, on a typical New York football-hockey Sunday, another strange thing happened at the Jim Brennan memorial seats. Before the game, I was approached by a man from Toronto who asked if we would exchange seats with him. His seats were as good as ours, maybe even better, being directly behind the Leafs bench; but to his chagrin, since he was traveling with the wife of one of the Leafs players, he could not, for obvious reasons, be seen in the seats he had acquired. My seats, while close to the ice, were at an angle such that they could not be seen from the players bench; I agreed to the trade, but always wondered how this couple dealt with being seen by Leaf players while on the ice; but that was not my worry.

Montreal,   January 22, 1966

GAME

270 Montreal Forum

Detroit Red Wings at Montreal Canadiens

The Montreal Canadiens always had a great mystique; whenever possible I followed their games on television and radio, even listening to French language broadcasts when I couldn't find an English version; but I had never been to Montreal, not to the city, nor to the Forum. Two things most impressed me about my first visit; even though my seat was fairly high, the building's steep slope afforded an intimate feeling throughout; secondly, every aspect of the game was under intense scrutiny from fifteen thousand knowing, caring pairs of eyes; every play was met with the appropriate crowd reaction; while New York and Boston fans were for the most part fairly hockey-savvy, one could find many with little knowledge of the game, who were rinkside for a social occasion; not so on St. Catherine Street, where a Canadiens game was a serious, almost religious event; I toured as much of Montreal as possible, paying little attention to the snow that fell heavily all weekend, closing the airport; my trip back to New York involved sixteen hours on a bus and a 4am Monday arrival at Port Authority; but I had no regrets; a true NHL fan has to go to the Montreal Forum.

New York,   February 12, 1966

GAME

Madison Square Garden **274**

Boston Bruins at New York Rangers

Toronto,   February 12, 1966

GAME

Maple Leaf Gardens **275**
Detroit Red Wings at Toronto Maple Leafs

Soon after my Montreal trip, I set aside a weekend for games in Toronto and Detroit. Late Saturday afternoon I flew to Toronto and headed straight for the action on Carleton Street. Saturday night in Toronto is synonymous with Leafs hockey but his was bigger than most; with Gordie Howe and the Red Wings in town, a Leafs-Wings battle for first place in the six team NHL was a huge event; fortunately I picked up a "gray", paying $12 for a ticket marked $2 and feeling happy to obtain it. The dilution of hockey was demonstrated to me about ten years later right there on Carleton Street when I bought a ticket marked $12 for $2 from an owner thrilled to be able to dispose of it; Maple Leaf Gardens is a perfect hockey building; to this day I love going there, and now that it is the only NHL building older than I am, it is my most frequent stop on the NHL tour. The Leafs are, to say the least, not the perennial Cup contenders of the past, but a night at the historic Gardens is still a great experience.

FAVORITE HOCKEY ARENAS:

All-Time:

1. Chicago Stadium
2. Montreal Forum
3. Boston Garden
4. Spectrum, Philadelphia
5. Met Center, Minnesota

Current Arenas:

1. Maple Leaf Gardens, Toronto
2. San Jose Arena
3. Great Western Forum, Los Angeles
4. Madison Square Garden, New York
5. Civic Arena, Pittsburgh

Detroit, February 13, 1966

GAME

276  Olympia Stadium

Montreal Canadiens at Detroit Red Wings

I had all day Sunday to get to Detroit so a leisurely bus ride with stops in numerous Ontario towns fit both my schedule and my budget; I loved the Olympia immediately; it was from the same mold as the two Gardens, Boston and Madison Square, and had the same intimacy whether rinkside or in a balcony. The Wings fans were devoted and intense, perhaps a little more so this night because the bleu, blanc and rouge were in town. As in New York, Boston and Chicago, Sunday was hockey night in the U.S. and the most special Sundays in each of those cities were those seven each winter when the Canadiens came to town; Montreal was always among the strongest teams in the six team NHL, but beyond that had an unmatched flair and tradition of excellence that brought out the biggest crowds for their road games; I sat rinkside in Olympia this night, just as I did at Madison Square Garden; in that sense it was similar to most of my Sunday evenings, only the Wings, not the Rangers were the home team. With the Rangers not scheduled at home this night, I was quite pleased I'd gone to the trouble to get to Detroit, and pleased that the game was played quickly enough for me to make the 10pm flight back to New York.

New York, February 23, 1966

GAME

278 Madison Square Garden

Detroit Red Wings at New York Rangers

Over the years, dozens of people, male and female, joined me at the Garden for Rangers games; some, like Jim Brennan, will never forget the experience; other names I recently found scribbled on an old 1965-66 schedule are people I've completely lost track of. My date for this Wednesday evening was a young schoolteacher who was moving to California at the end of the school year. I too was scheduled to transfer to the firm's San Francisco office within a matter of weeks; this was our first date and the first of about three hundred games Ellen would attend with me; we were married in 1967, divorced in 1985; she now lives happily in Long Island with her third husband. I don't think she goes to Ranger games any more.

GAME
Cow Palace 🏒 289

Victoria Maple Leafs at San Francisco Seals

I had heard of the Cow Palace, as it had been the venue for some Warriors basketball and a number of boxing matches. But until I went there, I did not appreciate how a building intended for livestock shows could be adapted into a functional indoor sports facility; nonetheless, it was less than big league; sitting on a street in Daly City just south of the city line, the Cow Palace reminded me of the ancient "Big E" back in West Springfield, Mass; but I had to accept that one of the consequences of my assignment to San Francisco was leaving big time hockey behind; the other major league sports were here, but from a hockey standpoint, I'd definitely been sent to the minors.

Los Angeles,   May 18, 1966

GAME
Dodger Stadium ⚾ 293

San Francisco Giants at Los Angeles Dodgers

Eleven years after my friends and I ventured unescorted and unarmed into upper Manhattan, I was once again watching the Giants and Dodgers; this time it was on a beautiful night at Dodger Stadium, with Sandy Koufax pitching a shutout for the Dodgers. Supposedly, the intensity of the Brooklyn-New York hatred had been transferred to the West Coast and, I guess, now that I was a San Franciscan, I should hate the Dodgers or at least root for the Giants against them. Yet I find it impossible to dislike anything about Dodger Stadium or the team; the Dodger tradition and organization has such a continuity of excellence that while I may not call myself a Dodger fan, Dodger games, in person and on television, give me more enjoyment than most others. Today, teams build ballparks (usually with taxpayer money) then declare them inadequate and threaten to move. Yet here is a stadium, now thirty-five years old (built when even the largest dictionary did not contain the term "luxury box") that remains the best in baseball. I still go to Dodger Stadium every chance I get.

San Francisco, July 4, 1966

GAMES

294, 295 Candlestick Park

(doubleheader) St. Louis Cardinals at San Francisco Giants

My daughter, Mary Beth, now twenty-five, remarked recently that she couldn't picture me living in San Francisco in the sixties. I assured her that I loved it and lived just as I did in New York, going to work and going to sports; her stereotypical San Franciscan wearing flowers in their hair, living in Haight-Ashbury and observing the LSD diet was more myth than reality. The closest I got to Haight-Ashbury was Kezar Stadium; during the summer I frequented Candlestick Park, mostly on weekends since the insufferable evening cold at Giants games is well documented. The fourth of July schedule was ideal; the doubleheader started at ten thirty in the morning, so I saw eighteen innings of baseball and was heading over the Golden Gate to the comparative warmth of my Marin County home before the daily late afternoon frigid wind arrived.

Minneapolis, July 16, 1966

GAME

298 Metropolitan Stadium

Washington Senators at Minnesota Twins

I told Mary Beth that her Mom and I spent a weekend in Minnesota in the sixties; what did you do, she asked kiddingly, go to the Mall of America? It was her subtle way of suggesting that until the megamall arrived a couple of years ago, we would have had difficulty finding anything worthwhile to do. As I pondered my answer, I realized that we had indeed gone to the Mall of America, or at least the exact spot where the Mall now sits. And, as far as I'm concerned the land was better used in 1966 than today; the world has enough malls, but can always use another fine outdoor baseball stadium. The Met, as it was known, was one of my favorite baseball parks, triple decked around home plate, double decked in left field, with single level seating down the foul lines; it looked as though it were built piecemeal, which it was, sections of steel added as needed to accommodate the expanding needs of baseball and football configurations. It was not Fenway Park or Dodger Stadium, but for as long as it lasted it was an outstanding place to watch a game. Put an outdoor stadium like the Met in Minneapolis today, liberating the Twins from their domed football stadium home, and baseball will again thrive in Minnesota; but if the natives can't figure out how to provide the Twins with a decent stadium, my adopted home area will take a big step toward becoming the wasteland my family and friends in New York mistakenly believe it already is.

San Francisco,   September 11, 1966

GAME

Kezar Stadium 299

Minnesota Vikings at San Francisco 49ers

If I have a favorite football team, it is the 49ers; this is in part because of the team's rich tradition of entertaining football dating back to the All America Conference years 1946 to 1949; in addition, my bond with the 49ers traces to 1966 at Kezar Stadium; it was here that I first obtained and paid for my own season tickets to any team. My friend Jerry Vetromile took over my rights when I left the Bay Area, and he and his family remain avid 49er fans to this day. One had to put in great effort to go to a Niners game at Kezar; parking wasn't just scarce, it didn't exist; neighborhood residents had difficulty finding parking on the street, so sixty thousand Sunday visitors really had to scramble; the bench seats were not built to accommodate wide-body humans, but many showed up anyway. Late in the season, the monsoon rains created a risk of drowning; and at all games, smashed (but always first emptied) liquor bottles were a serious hazard, especially in the fourth quarter. The fans were intense, but each in their own way; one man near us had a separate seat for his portable liquor cabinet; another not only kept score but assigned each member of his party chores in their own scorebook; one charted the defense, one the special teams, etc. No admittance unless eccentric; Kezar was truly a special place.

San Francisco,   October 21, 1966

GAME

Civic Auditorium 305

Detroit Pistons at San Francisco Warriors

San Franciscans derive a smugness from the belief that theirs is not just the best city in the world, but the only one worth inhabiting. In the mid-sixties the Warriors captured that attitude perfectly with a logo featuring the image of the Golden Gate Bridge, beneath which read two words: "THE CITY". Not just any city, not New York or Chicago, but THE city in which the Warriors played; and this Warrior team could play in any city; led by superstars Rick Barry and Nate Thurmond, they were the class of the NBA; their home games were played in several Bay Area arenas, but their principal home was the Civic Auditorium downtown; square in the midst of Civic Center, near the Opera House, Public Library and City Hall the austere stone building might, from outward appearances, house the Motor Vehicle Bureau; but inside it was a throwback to NBA arenas I had heard of as a child, tiny gyms in Sheboygan, Syracuse, Moline and others long since purged from the NBA map. Here, in the world's most sophisticated city performed the NBA's best team in a circa 1950 building. I loved it.

Los Angeles, November 26, 1966

GAME

315 Los Angeles Memorial Coliseum

Notre Dame at Southern California

I had not really followed college football for several years;
but Notre Dame isn't just any college, and in California,
neither is USC; in Los Angeles for the weekend, we saw
the Lakers at the Sports Arena Friday night and felt compelled to return the next
day to the adjacent Coliseum for the traditional match between the Trojans and
Fighting Irish; it's a good thing the game wasn't important to me; pilots landing at
LAX had a clearer view of the game; we were in the East end zone, or more
correctly about 150 yards east of the East end zone, near the Nevada border; the
Coliseum has since been downsized and reconfigured to eliminate these seats;
Notre Dame romped, 51-0; I'm glad we were there, I guess.

Boston, February 11, 1967

GAME

336 Boston Garden

Montreal Canadiens at Boston Bruins

I n my half century following the NHL, there has never been as dominating a
player as Bobby Orr. A Bruins rookie in 1967, at age eighteen he was already
taking charge of the game; the Bruins were rising from mediocrity to dynasty;
while they missed the playoffs in Orr's rookie spring of 1967, the Bruins were
competitive; led by Orr, whose bursts out of his own zone, gathering speed through
the center ice area, changed the whole way defensemen play, the Bruins were for
the first time in my memory a truly exciting team. Orr showed his toughness this
night with a quick knockdown of Montreal tough guy Ted Harris; many of my
games in Boston were more important in the standings, but none more memorable
than the first sighting of Bobby Orr.

New York, February 28, 1967
GAMES

Madison Square Garden 340, 341

Los Angeles Lakers vs. Detroit Pistons

San Francisco Warriors at N Y Knickerbockers

Hard as it is to believe today, most NBA teams had difficulty selling tickets until the last decade. Few if any teams played all their home games in their home city; a half dozen or so home games would be played in another team's arena to create an NBA doubleheader; the doubleheader was quite common in the fifties, and had disappeared completely by 1970; in the late sixties, with only ten teams in the league, it was possible to see forty percent of the league's players in a single evening. Talk about getting your five dollars worth.

San Francisco, March 26, 1967
GAME

Cow Palace 346

Los Angeles Lakers at San Francisco Warriors

My wife Ellen was a devout Catholic, had been in the convent and taught in Catholic schools; it is fair to assume that in her mind early Easter Sunday morning did not normally involve sports. But the NBA playoffs were televised at 2pm Eastern time, meaning the Warriors and Lakers squared off at 11am Easter morning; there's nowhere I'd rather have been, so our first Easter together was spent worshiping sports, just the way I liked it.

Palm Springs, March 29, 1967
GAME

Angels Stadium 347

Cleveland Indians at California Angels

A sure sign of spring is the arrival of exhibition baseball on the radio; it could be cold and snowy in New York, but the soft purr of the crowd at the Florida or Arizona ball park even sounded warm, and signaled that the weather would soon turn for the better in the Northeast. For the past twenty years I've been a regular at Florida spring training parks, but my first taste of spring baseball came in Palm Springs on a hot, dry, beautiful relaxed afternoon as the Indians (who had yet to become a glamour team) battled the Angels (who of course never have had any fans of their own).

Oakland, September 3, 1967

GAME

357 Oakland-Alameda County Coliseum

San Francisco 49ers at Oakland Raiders

The pre-season football game didn't count in the standings; the coaches were concerned solely about their team's readiness for NFL play (the 49ers) and AFL games (the Raiders) a week later. The football game was incidental; this was the smug establishment (the 49ers) against Hell's Angels (the Raiders); the confident, superior NFL against the brash, upstart AFL; the sanctimonious city against the blue-collar East Bay, in short Good versus Evil. Our 49ers won; looking back, I wonder how we got out alive.

Philadelphia, October 28, 1967

GAME

367 Spectrum

Detroit Red Wings at Philadelphia Flyers

The NHL expanded from six to twelve teams in the fall of 1967; teams played twenty-four games against the opposite conference, fifty against their fellow Eastern Conference (Original Six) or Western Conference (known for years as expansion teams) rivals. None of the six new teams were immediate box office successes; supply and demand for tickets, throughout the league, re-calibrated quickly, depending on whether the game involved expansion or Original Six teams. Traditionalists such as myself were wary of the Western Conference, inasmuch as the teams' rosters were stocked exclusively with marginal NHL players or veteran minor leaguers. I was familiar with many players from the American and Western Leagues, and felt somewhat shortchanged that two of the annual visits of the Rangers' Original Six rivals would be replaced by teams named Penguins, North Stars, Kings, Seals, Flyers and Blues. The first Original Six team to appear in Philadelphia was the Red Wings and I was there to check out the Flyers and their new arena; within five years the Flyers were the hottest team in Philly and a role model for any expansion franchise, but this month they toiled in obscurity; their games were not even on the radio; with an established team in town, the crowd swelled to about ten thousand, compared to typical crowds of about five thousand for games against fellow expansionists; to my pleasant surprise, I loved the new building, found it most accessible and comfortable; it was my first step toward becoming a Flyers fan.

GAME

Spectrum 384

New York Rangers at Philadelphia Flyers

We went to sports on Easter, why not on Christmas? Very few games are scheduled on Christmas anymore, but years ago the NHL played a full schedule (usually before full houses) on Christmas night; by now we were living in an apartment in Manhattan, and had spent the day with Ellen's relatives in upstate Schenectady. I made sure we arrived home by 5pm; I dared not reveal my motive until we were back in New York. I needed to allow time to get to the Spectrum for a 7pm face off between the Flyers and Rangers. I couldn't let the day go completely to waste.

New York, February 18, 1968

GAME

Madison Square Garden 400

Philadelphia Flyers at New York Rangers

The "new Garden" above the commuter terminal at Penn Station had been hyped as the next wonder of the world. The aging triple decked facility at Eighth and 49th would be replaced by a modern arena where seats would rise in a single bowl from ice level to the ceiling, with sections identified by color; to this day, even though all seats in the Garden are purple, the various levels are still commonly referred to as reds, oranges, yellows, greens and (worst of all, in the remote balcony area) blues. I studied brochures, seat plans and price scales and signed up for season tickets to the Rangers (first row yellows, right on the corner) and Knicks (center court yellows). I felt prudent; I got the best of the five dollar seats; reds were available, but at seven dollars seemed much too pricey. (Look for a red for a Knicks game nowadays and see how far seven bucks goes). I fully expected that the new Garden would be vastly superior and add to my hockey enjoyment. I couldn't have been more wrong; the sight lines were such that only in the first several rows could one see the ice closest to the near boards; so from my carefully chosen seats, fifteen rows up from the ice, I see a cluster of players scramble to the corner directly beneath us and VANISH COMPLETELY! It was the next step toward becoming a Flyers fan; that fall, I got season tickets at the Spectrum, where you could see the game.

New York,   February 20, 1968
GAMES

401, 402 Madison Square Garden

Chicago Bulls vs. Detroit Pistons

San Francisco Warriors
at New York Knickerbockers

T he much smaller surface permitted an excellent view of the entire basketball court. The blind spots so maddening to hockey fans did not obstruct any part of the Knicks game; the Garden sight lines are perfect for basketball, so Knicks fans never really understood what the fuss was about; but older hockey fans, to this day, miss the old Garden. The NBA doubleheader this night was played before what was then the largest crowd in the NBA's twenty-two year history; the Knicks and Warriors played an overtime thriller; a great way to open what is still the most sophisticated of NBA arenas, where fans are the most knowledgeable in the NBA, showing better understanding of the game than some players do; the crowd anticipates plays most perceptively; a player from either team, making the wrong move at the Garden will always hear about it from the crowd even more quickly than from his coach.

New York,   March 3, 1968
GAMES

405, 406 Madison Square Garden

Oakland Seals vs. Philadelphia Flyers

Chicago Blackhawks at New York Rangers

T he Spectrum, completed barely in time to launch the Flyers franchise, fell victim to a late February windstorm that blew the roof off the building; the Flyers had to finish the final month of their home schedule elsewhere; eventually they found a second home in Quebec City, but their immediate crisis was a home game scheduled for national television just two days after the catastrophe; the game was moved to Madison Square Garden; in an effort to show a sizeable crowd on television, ticketholders for the evening's Rangers evening game were admitted free to the Flyers afternoon game; it was a ten minute walk from my apartment to the Garden; two games, no parking or gasoline costs (and a refund from the Flyers for my Spectrum tickets). It was the closest to my beloved NBA doubleheaders that the NHL ever offered.

New York, April 4, 1968

GAME

Madison Square Garden 416

Chicago Blackhawks at New York Rangers

He was old, crude, nasty and in every way objectionable. His season tickets were in my row at the new Garden. Shortly before the end of each period, and several minutes after the start of the next he would push by, muttering: "Penn Bar, Penn Bar, coming through"; we learned he spent intermissions at a saloon named Penn Bar just outside the Garden having a couple of quick cocktails. No one knew his real name, but he quickly became known as Penn Bar. He was as annoying as the blind spot in the corner of the rink, and he never missed a game (or an intermission highball). This night the Rangers-Hawks playoff match was overshadowed by news spreading throughout the Garden that Martin Luther King had been assassinated; the crowd was shocked into silence; but not Penn Bar; his intermission exit was punctuated by unspeakably insensitive comments about the late Dr. King as well as the usual "Penn Bar, Penn Bar" message. My daughter once worked near Penn Station; visiting her office I looked up the block and there was a neon sign still burning brightly at Eighth and 31st ...PENN BAR... and it all came back to me. The place lives, but I'm sure Penn Bar the person has long since departed for the great redneck saloon in the sky. It's safe to say Will Rogers never met Penn Bar.

Philadelphia, April 13, 1968

GAME

Spectrum 419

St. Louis Blues at Philadelphia Flyers

The roof safely back on the Spectrum, the Flyers are in the playoffs, and filling their new building for a first round showdown with the St. Louis Blues; rookie coach Scotty Bowman has taken a unique approach with the Blues, bringing a number of veterans (Doug Harvey and Dickie Moore come to mind) out of retirement, bringing many years of Stanley Cup championship experience to a first year expansion team. Two of the greatest goaltenders ever, Jacques Plante and Glenn Hall, along with a tough defense led by Noel Picard and the Plager brothers, gave the Flyers all they could handle; while the Flyers won this particular battle, they were about to lose the playoff series. Flyers players were completely intimidated as teammate Claude LaForge was beaten into semi-consciousness by Picard; a fan threw a smoke bomb on to the ice during the brawl, creating a distraction that settled things down for a while. Flyers brass vowed that never again would a team come into the Spectrum and beat up the Flyers. The Broad Street Bullies were born that night; ever since, the Flyers have always been known for exceptional effort and toughness, particularly on Spectrum ice.

Chicago, October 11, 1968

GAME

424 Chicago Stadium

St. Louis Blues at Chicago Blackhawks

At the start of the 1968-69 season I decided that all twelve NHL teams, including the six expansion teams, were worth watching and I should plan to see at least one home game in each city. New York and Philadelphia were no problem, since I had season tickets to both, but the rest of the itinerary took planning; most of my work was in New York State, so the trips had to fit into weekends and around a holiday trip to Hawaii. This first stop, on Opening Night, was at Chicago Stadium, the only one of the "Original Six" arenas I had never visited; now, nearly 30 years later, I can say without equivocation, that there never was, and never will be, a more exciting, electric and fan friendly place to attend a hockey game. Chicago Stadium combined the history and tradition of Toronto and Montreal with the raucous enthusiasm of New York and Boston, and took both to a new level; it was at once the largest NHL building and the most intimate; people were jammed in everywhere. two balconies hung at steep angles over the ice so even the most distant fan felt a part of the game; the noise was such that a casual conversation was rarely possible; you could hear everybody, collectively, but you could hear nobody, individually; as if it needed more noise, the giant organ reverberated throughout the arena; this building was the best, bar none; it is a shame it is gone.

Philadelphia, November 7, 1968

GAME

437  Spectrum

St. Louis Blues at Philadelphia Flyers

I don't tend to remember individual performances and statistics; sometimes I quickly forget the final score, and rarely remember who scored all the goals or touchdowns. But this night was different; only once before had an NHL player scored six goals in a game, and that was long before I followed the game. This night at the Spectrum the Flyers were humiliated 8-0; the score was not news, after all the Hawks would come in ten weeks later and beat the Flyers 12-0; the news was that six of the goals were scored by Red Berenson, the one time Rangers forward picked up by the Blues in the expansion draft; it was the greatest individual performance I've ever seen in an NHL game.

San Diego,   December 25, 1968

GAME

San Diego Sports Arena **461**

Phoenix Roadrunners at San Diego Clippers

14   9   3

SEC.   ROW   SEAT

LOGE

San Diego Int'l. Sports Arena

DEC. 25 - $4.00
1968 - 8:00 P.M.

If it's Christmas I must be at a game; mostly, I'm bored by holidays because the sports world slows almost to a halt; our winter vacation will be spent in Hawaii, following an NHL stop in Los Angeles. We find ourselves in San Diego for Christmas, a city celebrating the return of the officers and crew of the Pueblo from their captivity by the North Vietnamese. Relatives were reunited with crew members in emotional proceedings at the downtown El Cortez Hotel. We watched for a while, but soon I had seen enough, particularly since the Western Hockey League had a matinee scheduled at the Sports Arena.

Los Angeles,   January 1, 1969

GAME

The Forum   **463**

St. Louis Blues at Los Angeles Kings

Rarely do I buy tickets in advance for an individual game; it is sort of a superstition, that the possession of tickets will be a jinx and something will happen to alter my schedule. For New Year's night 1969, however, I should have picked up tickets; our flight from Hawaii ran three hours late; even though the Forum is barely three miles from LAX the game was in the second period when I got to the arena; there were thousands of empty seats, but the Kings box office was closed; I went to every building entrance trying to buy a ticket, but no one could sell me one; when a side door opened and a photographer exited, I darted through and disappeared into the stands; it was the only time I ever sneaked into a game without a ticket, but the Kings gave me no choice; the game was memorable in that two aging but still great goalies, Terry Sawchuk of the Kings and Jacques Plante of the Blues, both posted shutouts, producing the rarest of NHL outcomes, a scoreless tie.

Minneapolis, Jan. 4, 1969

GAME

465 Metropolitan Sports Center

Boston Bruins at Minnesota North Stars

O ur Hawaiian vacation over, we headed home to New York, stopping in Minnesota long enough for my first visit to the home of the North Stars; I was impressed (as I would remain until the day the arena was blown to bits to make room for more Mall of America parking) with the simple functionality of Met Center; it was built quickly, economically, and specifically for hockey; many other events came to the Met, but it was first and foremost a hockey rink; for its quarter century lifetime, the Met was as good a building for viewing an NHL game as any in the league. My goal of completing the twelve team circuit was nearly complete; only Toronto remained, and it was quite easy to fit in a mid-week game at the Gardens; much of my work in those days was in upstate New York; a side trip to Toronto on the way to or from Rochester, Syracuse or Buffalo became something of a habit for the next several years.

Montreal, June 28, 1969

GAME

493 Jarry Park

Philadelphia Phillies at Montreal Expos

M ore than any other sport, baseball, to be appreciated fully, requires an understanding of history and traditions; until now, all the parks I'd visited had been special, majestic places where a larger than life ballfield appeared at the end of a runway from under the stands. A major league park would never be mistaken for a neighborhood playground. Until now. Jarry Park, home of the expansion Montreal Expos, was a city park, complete with a public swimming pool behind the right field fence; expanded to increase capacity to borderline major league proportions, Jarry still had more the feeling of a street festival than a major league game. Yet these were true major leaguers playing in this French neighborhood north of downtown and east of St. Laurent. The fans knew and respected the game, but expressed themselves differently than in the United States, with much singing and dancing in the aisles during the games. After a while, I got to like the place and actually missed it after the Expos left. I especially missed Jarry after I went to an Expos game at Olympic Stadium.

GAME
Yale Bowl 495

New York Jets at New York Giants

Anthropologists would confirm that Jet fans are all descended from Giant fans. Playing in different leagues, the Giants in the NFL, the Jets in the AFL, they had never played a game against each other; but now the two leagues were planning a merger and already playing inter-league exhibition games. The Giants are on the decline, and the upstart Jets most recent game was their stunning upset of the Baltimore Colts in Super Bowl III; so the ingredients were present for the most hyped exhibition game in football history; the Jets, despite their Super Bowl victory, had more to prove against the presumed superior, established Giants, and dominated the game in a sold out, steaming Yale Bowl. Objectively, the game meant nothing; but the term "bragging rights" was born this day when Giant and Jet fans alike headed seventy-five miles northeast to New Haven, all pumped into a frenzy for a meaningless exhibition game.

West Lafayette, Indiana; September 27, 1969

GAME
Ross-Ade Stadium 498

Notre Dame at Purdue

College fans tend to behave in a more civilized manner than their pro counterparts, possibly because nearly all of them either attended college or want others to believe they did; therefore their harmless hysteria takes the form of mindless obedience to unintelligible cheerleaders and wardrobe colors too hideous to imagine; I have nothing against Purdue; and, while Notre Dame is as close to being "America's Team" as any, I have no particular attachment to the Fighting Irish either; what I remember most is the size of the Purdue campus, and how the distance from all parking spaces to all parts of the stadium has been maximized. The Boilermakers beat the Irish, cause for serious celebration in this part of Indiana. I just wanted to get out of town.

Barrie, Ontario;   September 30, 1969

GAME

499  **Barrie Arena**

Detroit Red Wings at Los Angeles Kings

The family (all two and seven ninths of us) got a jump on the 1969-70 NHL season with a swing through some training camps in Ontario. The appearance of Gordie Howe and the Wings jammed most of Barrie's population into the local arena, even though the game was just an exhibition. After the game, we returned to our Toronto hotel, and at midnight, my six year military reserve "career" expired. Returning to the United States I was interrogated at the border to verify that I was not a Vietnam-war draft evader sneaking back from Canada; at Niagara Falls we were asked if we were honeymooners; in retrospect, both were more plausible explanations of what we were doing in Canada than the truth, New Yorkers following NHL teams' training camps.

 FAVORITE FOOTBALL STADIUMS:

1. Giants Stadium, New Jersey

2. Pro Player Park, Miami

3. Arrowhead Stadium, Kansas City

4. Houlihan's Stadium, Tampa

5. Cleveland Stadium

6. Metrodome, Minneapolis

7. Aloha Stadium, Honolulu

8. Orange Bowl, Miami

9. 3Com Park, San Francisco

10. R F K Stadium, Washington

Chapter IV

The 70's

Hockey Is My Passion

I spent the seventies in Long Island, with my consulting practice based in Manhattan, but increasingly involving travel throughout North America. My habit of seeing at least one NHL game in each city continued through the seventies, becoming especially challenging as the league went from twelve teams at the start of the decade to twenty-one at the end; all other sports faded from my attention, although I did visit all the major league ball parks and began spending Spring Training in Florida; by the end of the decade I was a Vice President of the consulting firm, and had two children who were starting to accompany me to games; during the seventies I went to 989 games, 729 of them hockey and another 223 baseball; 532 games were in New York State, 134 in Pennsylvania, and the remainder distributed among seventeen states and four Canadian provinces.

GAME

Boston Garden  521

Detroit Red Wings at Boston Bruins

The Bruins dynasty was the class of the NHL; locating Bruins tickets was as tough as finding pork chops in Miami Beach, so when I got a call on a Saturday afternoon telling me that four loges were waiting on Causeway Street, three friends and I were in the car; never mind the snowstorm forecast for New York; never mind my month old son John at home; after all, his mother wasn't coming to Boston with us; when you could get to see Orr, Esposito, Sanderson, Hodge, Cheevers and company at home you seized the moment; it was probably the most dominating, yet most exciting hockey roster ever.

Chicago, April 8, 1970

GAME

Chicago Stadium 535

Detroit Red Wings at Chicago Blackhawks

It became known as the 4-2 series, as the Hawks won all four games by that same score; for me, it will be remembered as my first of many Stanley Cup playoff games at my all time favorite hockey building. The capacity was listed as 16,666; perhaps that's how many fans were seated, but there looked to be and additional ten thousand standing; people were actually standing on ledges against the wall of the building high ABOVE the second balcony; how they got there I'll never know, but their willingness to be there confirmed the incalculable passion of the Blackhawk fan.

New York,   November 28, 1970

GAME

563 Madison Square Garden

Boston Bruins at New York Rangers

GAME

564 Madison Square Garden

Milwaukee Bucks at New York Knickerbockers

There were many days of Rangers-Knicks doubleheaders at the Garden, and this was one of the best; Ranger historians will confirm that the 1970-71 team was perhaps the strongest ever; this afternoon they played the defending champion Bruins to a 3-3 tie; the evening at the Garden was if anything even more thrilling as the Knicks surged from behind to capture a one point victory over the Milwaukee Bucks, powered by rookie Lew Alcindor (later known as Kareem Abdul-Jabbar).

Montreal,   February 11, 1971

GAME

590 Montreal Forum

Minnesota North Stars at Montreal Canadiens

This season, as always, I would make the NHL circuit, but would do so all in the month of February; the stop in Montreal was the start of a weekend binge of seven games in seven cities in four days; it was a classic in Canadiens history as it was the night of Jean Beliveau's five hundredth career goal; Beliveau was as complete a hockey player as I'd ever seen; tough yet elegant, a winner, the last link to the Canadien dynasties of the fifties and sixties; it was a privilege to be in the Forum for the momentous accomplishment.

Pittsburgh, February 13, 1971

GAME

Civic Arena **592**

Chicago Blackhawks at Pittsburgh Penguins

St. Louis, February 13, 1971

GAME

St. Louis Arena **593**

New York Rangers at St. Louis Blues

Two games in a day in different cities was a fairly common occurrence (forty-eight times in my fifty year journey); this connection was complicated by a snowstorm; my arrival in Pittsburgh was by overnight Greyhound from Buffalo; the 5pm to St Louis took off in a blinding snowstorm; the home teams won both games by a one goal margin, but I recall little about the games, and lots about the tough travel connections.

Minneapolis, February 14, 1971

GAME

Metropolitan Sports Center **594**

Pittsburgh Penguins at Minnesota North Stars

Chicago, February 14, 1971

GAME

Chicago Stadium **595**

Vancouver Canucks at Chicago Blackhawks

The connections were somewhat easier; a pre-dawn flight from St Louis to Minnesota and a 5pm Minneapolis to Chicago; the North Stars game was memorable for the raging tantrum thrown by Jude Drouin directed at referee Bruce Hood; Drouin was of course ejected; leaving the arena we noticed a police wagon outside; jokingly I suggested it was there for Drouin; far more likely, its customers would be some of the Paul Bunyan types whose idea of a good time was to bus in from Fargo, devour a case of Grain Belt and throw up on each other at a North Stars game; the eventual demise of the NHL in Minnesota was as attributable to downscale demographics as anything else; this was, to say the least, not a luxury box crowd. That evening, a tired hockey traveler had no trouble staying awake; raucous, festive Chicago Stadium was the best place in hockey to finish a ninety-six hour, seven game binge.

Detroit, February 28, 1971

GAME

602  Olympia Stadium

Pittsburgh Penguins at Detroit Red Wings

I t took the entire twenty-eight days of February, but the fourteen city NHL circuit was completed in a single month. I spent the afternoon watching the NHL on TV at a Detroit restaurant; as always, Olympia was an exciting place for a game; It may seem presumptuous for Detroiters to refer to their city as Hockeytown USA but they are entitled; support of the Red Wings never wavers, through thick and thin; Detroit has had more than its share of economic hardship, but the locals have always made support of their team a priority; no flimsy excuses about high ticket prices, or competition from college or high school hockey (all of which excuses could certainly be made in Detroit); the fans are hard core, probably the most knowledgeable in any American city.

Philadelphia, April 10, 1971

GAME

618  Veterans Stadium

Montreal Expos at Philadelphia Phillies

GAME

619 Spectrum

Chicago Blackhawks at Philadelphia Flyers

T he new home of the Phillies opened on a cold Saturday in April. The stadium was packed; three of the freezing crowd were my friends Bill Shannon and Dave Hynes and myself. Hynes and Shannon are two of the ultimate baseball purists who never leave until after the last man is out, and usually not for sometime after. Today was no exception; risking frostbite to tally all the scorecard stats, traffic had thinned before we left the ballpark; of course, I was in no hurry; while my friends headed for a train back to New York, I merely crossed the street to the Spectrum for a Stanley Cup 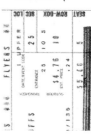 playoff game; it was the first of many Spectrum/Vet "doubleheaders" on America's most exciting sports street corner, the intersection of Broad and Pattison in South Philly.

GAME

Madison Square Garden  622

Chicago Blackhawks at New York Rangers

Without a doubt, it was the most exciting of all my NHL games; the Rangers faced elimination in game six of the Stanley Cup semi-finals; the Garden was in bedlam throughout as the teams played with great intensity finishing regulation time with two goals apiece. Close checking hockey, playoff hockey, the game as it was meant to be played; on to a second sudden death overtime; suddenly Stan Mikita fires a shot that hits the right goalpost, ricochets across the goal mouth, hits the left goalpost, and does not go in the net; the Rangers have missed elimination by an inch! In the THIRD overtime, Pete Stemkowski scores the game winner; it is 11:58pm on the clock but it is New Year's in Times Square in the Garden; strangers hug in the aisles, stumbling over semi-comatose drunks rolling down the stairs from the greens toward the yellows. It was all anti-climactic, however, as the Hawks took game seven in Chicago three days later, and the best ever Rangers team failed to advance to the Stanley Cup finals.

Long Island,   May 1, 1972

GAME

Nassau Coliseum 699

Virginia Squires at New York Nets

A new state of the art arena opens in Long Island, not ten minutes from my home; it will come to be known as the Mausoleum, a totally sterile, boring building occupied primarily by the hockey Islanders; the Islanders were formed later that summer, so the arena opened with the American Basketball Association's red, white and blue ball entering the basket with amazing frequency as the Squires and Nets put on a great two hundred eighty-two point spectacle. It was truly exciting, an arena a hundred miles closer to home than the Spectrum, and with better sight lines than the Garden; an NHL team would begin play in the fall; I gave up my Flyers season tickets and bought Islanders tickets. It was the worst trade in hockey history!

New York,   May 11, 1972

GAME
702 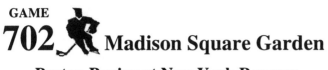 Madison Square Garden
Boston Bruins at New York Rangers

For the first time in twenty-two years the Rangers have advanced to the Stanley Cup finals; the curse of 1940 was about to be broken; or was it? For the first time, I saw the Stanley Cup carried around the ice by the victors; but it was Bruin captain Johnny Bucyk hoisting the Cup; we didn't realize it at the time but it would be still another twenty-two years of frustration for Rangers fans, before the Cup would find a home in the Garden.

Atlanta,   January 26, 1973

GAME
767  The Omni
Los Angeles Kings at Atlanta Flames

The New York Islanders and Atlanta Flames entered the NHL in 1972, so I added a new stop on my hockey itinerary, the "Magnificent Omni", housed the Flames in a fine new surroundings, luxurious by 1972 standards; the team was surprisingly competitive from the outset, and for the eight years hockey lasted in Atlanta, the fine arena and competitive team made trips to Atlanta quite enjoyable. I'm usually quite aware of what's going on at an event, and always bring binoculars and a radio to be sure I miss nothing. But this night I became completely befuddled by a sudden outburst of wild cheering and screaming by the Flames fans. I looked for action on the ice, fights in the stands, celebrities entering or leaving the building and found nothing at all; the radio was not reporting any news of interest, so what in the world was going on? I asked the person in the adjacent seat what all the commotion was about. "The organist is playing DIXIE", he replied.

GAME

Montreal Forum **814**

Philadelphia Flyers
at Montreal Canadiens

A Stanley Cup playoff game in the Forum is a major event; but when an upstart team in its sixth year of existence steals the opening game of a series at the Forum with an overtime victory, major hockey news is taking place. Call it a premonition, but in watching the Flyers that night I felt that this team would soon emerge as a powerhouse; they had a drive to excel, an indomitable spirit that made the team larger than its component parts; Montreal went on to take this series, but I came away believing that these Flyers would prove to be something quite special before long.

GAME

Spectrum **816**

Montreal Canadiens
at Philadelphia Flyers

The Flyers won at home to prolong the series but even the fanatics at the Spectrum hadn't caught on to the dynasty developing before their eyes; I'm never shy about making sports predictions; people forget the bad predictions quickly, but remember the good ones forever; on this night I ran into a business associate and his two young sons, all Flyer fans; I told the two boys the Flyers would win the Stanley Cup within a year; in May, 1974 my daring prediction came true; those boys are pushing forty years old now, but if we met again I'm sure they'd regard me as the Nostradamus of hockey.

New York,   October 8, 1973

GAME

835 Shea Stadium

Cincinnati Reds at New York Mets

Much of my summer in 1973 was spent at Shea Stadium, watching the improbable march of a .500 team toward the World Series; in a division characterized by parity or mediocrity, the Mets squeezed out first place and faced the heavily favored Reds in the League Championship Series; this sunny fall day at Shea will be best remembered for the Pete Rose-Bud Harrelson brawl at second base; the sight of one time Red great and current Met coach Roy McMillan racing in to join the brawl reminded me that the new hockey season was just a few days away.

Philadelphia,   October 11, 1973

GAME

838 🏒 Spectrum

Toronto Maple Leafs at Philadelphia Flyers

Kate Smith was the Flyers good luck charm. For no explainable reason, when her recording of God Bless America was substituted for the national anthem, the Flyers were nearly unbeatable at the Spectrum; hopes were high and the Spectrum full as the ever improving, intense, battling Bullies of Broad Street prepared for opening night. The mention of Kate Smith as the team lined up at center ice brought the fans to a Chicago Stadium-like frenzy; in all the screaming, some failed to notice they were being asked to stand and welcome not Kate Smith's recording, but Kate Smith LIVE at center ice; the surprise appearance of the portly old lady serenading the frenzied Spectrum with a live rendition of the Flyers lucky song solidified my feeling that a truly exceptional season was about to start. I was right.

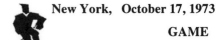

New York,   October 17, 1973

GAME

Madison Square Garden   **842**

St. Louis Blues at New York Rangers

GAME

Shea Stadium   **843**

Oakland Athletics at New York Mets

Thirteen years after I turned down the opportunity to go to the World Series in Pittsburgh, I finally got there, to all three games played at Shea Stadium in the 1973 series against Oakland. As familiar as I was with Shea, the World Series presented a logistical challenge; game four of the series started an hour and a half after the Rangers face off at the Garden; so I stayed two periods at the hockey game, and arrived at Shea in about the second inning of the World Series; as a result I had to park some distance away, behind one of the many nondescript industrial buildings in the area referred to in "The Great Gatsby" as the "Valley of the Ashes". After the game I returned to my car, calmly got in and started the ignition; then I noticed a scratching on the passenger side door; I looked into the eyes of the fiercest looking attack dog in this or any junkyard; frustrated that his dinner (me) had gotten away, he chased my speeding car all the way to Northern Boulevard; from then on, I got to Shea on time to park in the main lot.

A flat price flew me to all the sports I could find in the mid-seventies

Philadelphia, April 7, 1974

GAME

941 **Veterans Stadium**

New York Mets at Philadelphia Phillies

GAME

942 **Spectrum**

It was the final Sunday of the season; I had long since completed my annual "circuit" of the NHL's 14 arenas, but this afternoon's game at the Spectrum was my one hundredth regular season game of the 1973-74 hockey season; in today's diluted, slowed-down, dumb-downed NHL, watching a hundred games would be an appropriate penalty for a serious misdemeanor offense; in 1974, it was a joy! As I often did before Flyers or Sixers games at the Spectrum, catching batting practice and a few innings of the Phillies game across the street was my pre-game activity.

Philadelphia, May 14, 1974

GAME

953 **Veterans Stadium**

Montreal Expos at Philadelphia Phillies

GAME

954 **Spectrum**

Boston Bruins at Philadelphia Flyers

Another great evening at Broad and Pattison; batting practice and three innings at the Vet as a warm-up and a Stanley Cup finals battle between the Flyers and the Boston Bruins. The Flyers dominated, won the game 4-2 and were well on their way to their first, and most dramatic, Stanley Cup championship.

GAME

Astrodome 978

New York Mets at Houston Astros

During the 1974 baseball season, I made the rounds of all twelve National League ballparks; as a result, I visited the Astrodome for the first time; the place was nearly empty; while I sat close to the field, it just didn't feel like being in a baseball stadium; perhaps it would just take some getting used to, I thought; I was so wrong; having lived in Minnesota for the past ten years and been a regular at Twins games in the Metrodome, I am still no more comfortable with baseball in a dome than I was on this first visit.

Cincinnati, September 11, 1974

GAME

Riverfront Stadium 988

Atlanta Braves at Cincinnati Reds

The Braves and Reds met at Riverfront as I completed the National League circuit; visiting every stadium in baseball is more difficult than in hockey because of the risk of rainouts; fortunately, I encountered none, and none was likely tonight since no Reds game had been rained out since Riverfront opened in 1970. In the bottom of the fifth inning on a humid evening, Pete Rose scored for the Reds to tie the game 1-1; by the time Rose got to the dugout the skies opened with one of the heaviest rainstorms I've ever seen outside of Florida. The field soon became unplayable; but, just in the nick of time Rose's run made the game official; it went into the books as a 1-1 tie, and I headed for the airport having completed my tour of the National League.

Philadelphia,   October 12, 1974

GAME

1000  Spectrum

Buffalo Sabres at Philadelphia Flyers

Long Island,   October 12, 1974

GAME

1001 Nassau Coliseum

Kansas City Scouts at New York Islanders

A nother hockey doubleheader involved two landmarks on my sports journey; the afternoon game was my one thousandth sporting event; in the evening I took my son John, nearing his fifth birthday, to his first hockey game; he was especially excited because both teams' colors were blue, his favorite color, and because the Scouts jerseys had a horse on the front. It seems the Scouts logo impressed very few other people, certainly not many in Kansas City; within a couple of years, the Scouts were the Colorado Rockies and my son was a die-hard Islander fan.

Kansas City,   November 26, 1974

GAME

1026  Kemper Arena

Vancouver Canucks at Kansas City Scouts

A nother NHL expansion raised to sixteen the number of stops on my annual trip around the league; I went to one of the first games ever played by the Washington Capitals and was underwhelmed by the team, the arena, and by Landover Maryland; the other expansion stop was Kansas City, the team with the horse on the jersey; I knew the franchise was in trouble when I got in a cab at the downtown hotel and the driver had never heard of either Kemper Arena or the Kansas City Scouts; Kemper was a nice building, and probably still is; I've always enjoyed going to Kansas City, but Hockeytown USA it is not.

Los Angeles,   January 28, 1975

GAME

The Forum 🏒 1056

New York Rangers at Los Angeles Kings

At first it seemed a curse on the hockey traveler, a consulting project in El Paso, Texas; this might have caused serious disruption to my hockey season had I not found an efficient, but convoluted route home to New York; after a full day in El Paso, one could not make the last connection to New York; but going in the other direction, a 5pm out of El Paso would be in Los Angeles by 6, in plenty of time to get to the Forum; after the game, it was no problem to catch the red-eye to JFK and be back in New York in the morning. A Rangers-Kings match is especially enjoyable due to the large number of New York transplants in Southern California; hockey was not yet the sport of choice among the Angelinos, so visiting team partisans made up a high percentage of the Kings crowds. Sitting next to me was another New Yorker, about my age; we reminisced about the old Garden, and Ranger history; I never asked his name; a couple of years later I saw him on a popular TV series; he apparently was quite a well known actor; but in these pre-VCR, NHL every night years, television and movie stars were largely unrecognizable to me; I probably wouldn't have known Elvis if we left the building together; between my work and my hockey travels, little time remained for television.

New York,   April 11, 1975

GAME

Madison Square Garden 🏒 1080

New York Islanders at New York Rangers

The first round of NHL playoffs was best of three in those days, so some strange things could happen; the Islanders, in their third season had made the playoffs for the first time; the Rangers, while on the decline from their early seventies were still prohibitive favorites in this opening playoff round; the Rangers learned the hard way that if you let a game go into overtime you deserve whatever bad may happen to you; in the third and deciding game of the series, J.P.Parise scored eleven seconds into the overtime, leaving the Garden shocked and still; it was the beginning of the shifting of New York hockey power away from the Rangers and toward the Islanders.

Long Island, April 20, 1975

GAME

1084 Nassau Coliseum

Pittsburgh Penguins at New York Islanders

The Islanders magic that carried them to the first round upset of the Rangers seemed to be short-lived; Pittsburgh took the first three games of the next round and the Islanders seemed on their way to a four straight elimination from the playoffs this Sunday afternoon at home; even the most loyal of Islander fans had given up hope; but the youngest, my five year old son John remained completely optimistic; I explained how the Islanders would have to miraculously win four straight over the Penguins, and even if they did would have to face the defending Stanley Cup champion Flyers next; unimpressed by those long odds, John asked me in all seriousness, "Who will the Islanders play after the Flyers?" He nearly had the last laugh; the Islanders did come from down three games to none to take four in a row from the Penguins; against the Flyers they got down three again, but came back with three wins to force a seventh game; then their magic ran out, and the Flyers went on to the Stanley Cup finals.

Cincinnati, July 25, 1975

GAME

1098 Riverfront Stadium

Los Angeles Dodgers at Cincinnati Reds

People often ask me, "How do you get tickets to all these games?" It is a reasonable question, but I always point out that the tickets that can really be costly are not game tickets, but plane tickets. I've put far more effort into minimizing air travel costs than into finding game tickets, which are almost always obtainable the day of the game. In observation of America's bi-centennial anniversary in 1976, Allegheny Airlines (now known as US Airways) introduced a promotion known as Liberty Fare. Liberty Fare was offered from 1975 through about 1978 and permitted unlimited air travel on the Allegheny system for three weeks at a flat price that was roughly equal to a single round trip fare between, for example, New York and Chicago; the only catch was that the passenger was not supposed to depart or arrive at any given city more than once in the three week period, a constraint that could be easily observed. I had Liberty Passes of varied expiration dates in my possession almost continuously; my business travel covered much of the cost, leaving me with air transportation from the East Coast to all major cities as far west as St Louis and Minneapolis. Completing the hockey and baseball circuits became much simpler for the next several years; connecting in Pittsburgh enroute to sports became as routine as changing at Jamaica on the Long Island Railroad enroute to Madison Square Garden; I picked the best games and flew there on Allegheny. The Big Red Machine against the Dodgers at Riverfront was as good as the National League got in the mid-seventies; thanks to Liberty Fare, I was there.

Philadelphia, September 26, 1975
GAMES

Veterans Stadium ⚾ **1124, 1125**

(doubleheader)
New York Mets at Philadelphia Phillies

S ome fans are adamant about staying to the end of every game. Not me; I leave early to catch planes, beat traffic, or just because I've seen enough. Especially in hockey, the likelihood of something happening after my departure that I've not already seen many times is nil. But this strange night at the Vet, I was there until the bitter end of the doubleheader; the Phils won the first game in twelve innings on a disputed call; as the managers exchanged lineups for the second game, a huge argument erupted and Mets manager Roy Mc Millan was ejected at the home plate lineup exchange. Five and a half hours, three rain delays and another twelve innings later, the rest of the Mets (and I) left the Vet; the second game ended after 3am; probably less than a hundred fans were there for the Phils doubleheader sweep, and it was 5am before I was home in Long Island. Why on this night, for these unimportant late season games did I so uncharacteristically stay for the finish? No particular reason; I guess I was having a good time and had nowhere I needed to be early the next day.

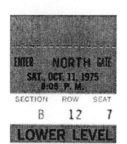

 Minneapolis, October 11, 1975
GAME

Metropolitan Sports Center **1128**

Philadelphia Flyers at Minnesota North Stars

A rmed with my Liberty Fare pass, I headed for Minnesota for the first weekend of the 1975-76 NHL season; a bigger attraction than the hockey game was the arrival, on Saturday afternoon of Joe Namath and the Jets at my hotel across from the stadium/hockey complex; hundreds crowded the hotel lobby awaiting the Jets arrival; naturally, their bus pulled up to a back door just as I was leaving through that door to walk across to the hockey arena; seeing the Jets come off the team bus meant absolutely nothing to me; how ironic that the hordes of zealots to whom it did matter never saw Joe Namath, while he walked right by me as I walked across the street to pick up a hockey ticket. The Cup champion Flyers drilled the North Stars 9-5, and lived up to the Broad Street Bully reputation on the physical side of the game as well.

Boston,   October 12, 1975

GAME

1129 ⚾ Fenway Park

Cincinnati Reds at Boston Red Sox

GAME

1130 🏒 Boston Garden

New York Islanders at Boston Bruins

Long before the Jets and Vikings took the field in Minnesota, I was on an early flight to Boston; by noon I was outside Fenway; on a misty day with intermittent rain, game three of what some believe to be the greatest World Series ever played was about to begin; I got a seat just a few rows off the field, slightly to the left of home plate; you could call the balls (not many) and strikes being thrown by Bill "Spaceman" Lee, pitching for the Sox. It was one of the relatively few times I've had a strong rooting interest in a game; but Red Sox fans have been selected to have an unusual capacity for disappointment; ever so close, but never quite there; a 3-2 Reds victory didn't wrap up the Series by any means, but it was an all too familiar omen. Of course, I stayed to the end of the game; I still had a couple of hours to kill before the Bruins and Islanders faced off at the Garden.

Atlanta,   December 26, 1975

GAME

1162 🏒 The Omni

Pittsburgh Penguins at Atlanta Flames

For thirty years I've carried a Pocket Flight Guide wherever I go; anyone who travels for business or pleasure will encounter bad weather, cancelled flights, and delays and need to be able to make quick adjustments to their itinerary; for many years, I used to take a sports trip each year between Christmas and New Year's, usually leaving New York on December 26. This time my first stop was Detroit, where the Wings were hosting the Islanders in an unusual 4pm start; from there I was going to Pittsburgh, Chicago and Minnesota the next several nights; but the trip got off to a bad start; my flight to Detroit was cancelled; no alternates were available; scanning the flight guide and the NHL schedule I found only one game I could get to that day, headed over to another airline and bought a ticket to Atlanta. Luck was on my side with that cancelled Detroit flight, since the Red Wings postponed their game; a heavy snowstorm had hit Detroit, but I was at an NHL game anyway; a midnight flight from Atlanta to Pittsburgh got me back on my original schedule.

Pittsburgh,   December 27, 1975

GAME

Three Rivers Stadium 1163

Baltimore Colts at Pittsburgh Steelers

GAME

Civic Arena 1164

Atlanta Flames at Pittsburgh Penguins

By arriving in Pittsburgh late Friday night, I got an unexpected bonus in my sports schedule, my first NFL post-season game; it was brutally cold at Three Rivers; the Steelers were on their way to a Super Bowl, dominated the game and won 28-10; it was not one of the most exciting sports events of my life, but it was something to do while waiting all day for the Flames-Penguins rematch at the Igloo that evening.

Oakland,   January 30, 1976

GAME

Oakland Coliseum Arena 1176

Montreal Canadiens at California Seals

My favorite hockey team is the three man team in the striped shirts. Over the years many of these un-derappreciated non-partisan game participants, referees and linesmen, have been good friends and good company along the NHL trail. One of the finest was John McCauley, as intelligent a person as I'd met in or out of sports; his quick mind made him one of the best officials ever, and while he died far too young he left a lasting impact on the game he loved. On this night in Oakland McCauley was presiding over an uncommon event, a well-played game in Oakland; the Seals were playing competitively against a Canadiens team which would go on to win the next four Stanley Cups. It had the makings of a classic match, if any of the spectators were knowledgeable enough to care. Encouraged by Crazy George, the buffoon who once, and only once, dared bang his silly drum close to my ear, the know-nothing locals put the blame for the Seals one goal defeat on McCauley; even the local radio focused on the refereeing, not the fine performance of the home team against the best team in hockey; so the raving East Bay mob went home blaming the league's top referee for the game's result. Now, of course, the league has expanded to lots of places where hockey-ignorant crowds scream madly at the top of their lungs, spurred on by all sorts of extraneous mascots and other theatrics. In that sense, the California Seals were twenty years ahead of their time.

Vancouver, February 20, 1976

GAME

1181  Pacific Coliseum

Minnesota North Stars at Vancouver Canuks

D uring the 1975-76 season I got to every NHL arena not
once, but at least twice; my two games in Vancouver were on consecutive
nights in February; both the St Louis and Minnesota teams were staying in
the same hotel; every time I crossed the lobby I was besieged by teenage vultures
begging me for an autograph; my age and body size, I suppose, were roughly
comparable to some NHL players of the day, but obviously the kids had no idea
whatsoever who I was; in all my years as a fan, I've never asked for an autograph,
or ever understood their appeal (except of course, that in recent years they have
become highly marketable to consumers with far more money than brains). The
young men became increasingly insistent; finally I obliged, gave each my scribbled
signature, leaving them to wonder what player they had been
chasing.

New York, May 20, 1976

GAME

1204 Shea Stadium

Philadelphia Phillies at New York Mets

GAME

1205 Yankee Stadium

Boston Red Sox at New York Yankees

I t was an unusual doubleheader, but an especially enjoyable one because of the teams involved; a 4pm start at Shea
Stadium between the Phillies and Mets left plenty of time
to zip across the Triboro Bridge for the 8pm renewal of the
storied Red Sox-Yankees rivalry; the visitors won both games,
and in the nightcap, Bill Lee and Graig Nettles were the main
event in a bench-clearing brawl.

Enter Gates 1 or 10 or 15

2 **94**

TIER   BOX
LOWER DECK BOX
$4.50
DETROIT TIGERS

RAIN CHECK

JUNE | TUESDAY
1 | — 1976 —
Good This Date Only
GAME THIS CHECK

Admit One—Subject to set forth on the back of ticket admission to a seat on this season only if season not
played on this date then
may be exchanged for a ticket of equal value

NO MONEY REFUNDED
THIS TICKET NON-TRANSFERABLE

Detroit, June 1, 1976

GAME

Tiger Stadium 1210

Milwaukee Brewers at Detroit Tigers

The 1976 season was the one and only in which I made the entire major league baseball tour, attending games in all twenty-four parks. In Detroit on business, I caught a game at Tiger Stadium, my first visit there. I knew it was my first Tiger home game but throughout the first few innings I had a sense of as Yogi would say "deja vu all over again". Finally it hit me; visualize a right field wall and screen where the Tiger Stadium double deck sits and there is an amazing resemblance to Ebbets Field; Tiger Stadium is a great stadium in its own right, but my visits are special because the ballpark stirs memories of my childhood in Brooklyn.

Enter Gate-**2**-MADISON

5 16 D 4

AISLE BOX ROW SEAT
BOX SEAT $12.50

SUN. OCT. | HOME GAME
24
1976
CHICAGO STADIUM

Chicago, October 24, 1976

GAME

Chicago Stadium 1255

St. Louis Blues at Chicago Blackhawks

The great Bobby Orr spent almost his entire career with the Bruins; plagued by knee injuries that would shorten the most brilliant career in hockey history, he signed as a free agent with the Hawks for the 1976-77 season; he would play only ten games in a Chicago uniform before injuries forced his retirement; this night he came out for the warmup in obvious pain, limping through the pre-game drills; I felt privileged to have seen him warm up, but was sure there was no way he could play. How wrong I was. Orr not only played, but led the Hawks to a 7-2 victory and was named the game's first star. It would be the last time I saw the greatest hockey player of our time.

Long Island,   April 7, 1977

GAME
1311  Nassau Coliseum

New York Islanders at Chicago Blackhawks

It is an oddity in NHL history; a Chicago Blackhawks home game in the opponent's building; so dubious were the Hawks playoff hopes in the spring of 1977 that their building was booked with concerts for the playoff dates; as a result, game two of the best of three opening round series with the Islanders could not be played at the Stadium; instead, the teams stayed in Long Island, switched benches and uniform colors and played a Blackhawks home game in New York; not surprisingly, there was no home ice advantage for the Hawks; the Islanders made it a two game sweep and sent the Hawks packing for the summer.

Toronto,   April 15, 1977

GAME
1314 Maple Leaf Gardens

Philadelphia Flyers at Toronto Maple Leafs

The Leafs grabbed two victories at the Spectrum and returned home for the next two games feeling confident of an upset of the favored Flyers. The Gardens, often a quiet and restrained place, was bedlam this Friday evening; with a 3-2 lead and only five minutes to play the Leaf faithful were near-delirious with joy; but the flow of the game was moving in the Flyers direction, and never has an NHL team played with as much heart and determination as the Flyers of the seventies; I boldly predicted to the Toronto fan next to me that the Leafs would not win another game in this series, not even tonight's. I was right; Rick MacLeish's overtime winner at the Gardens gave the Flyers the first of four straight victories and advancement to the Stanley Cup semi-finals. There they were much less successful, being swept by the equally gutsy Boston Bruins in four straight games.

War Memorial Auditorium 1317

Nova Scotia Voyageurs
at Rochester Americans

Like the teams, the officials compete for playoff position; having missed part of the season, McCauley was assigned to the American League for the playoffs; my schedule coincided with his at the ancient War Memorial in downtown Rochester; many fine players performed that night, particularly for the Nova Scotia Voyageurs, Montreal's top minor league affiliate. But the atmosphere was truly minor league; to my left was a woman with a cow-bell, reminiscent of Hilda Chester at Ebbets Field; everyone on the ice, as well as myself, would have preferred to be at an NHL playoff game; but the post-game festivities at our hotel were definitely big league; 7am came far too early, but my seven year old son had a morning soccer game, the first of many times in the next ten years when my business and sports schedules would also have to be coordinated with youth hockey and soccer commitments.

Three Rivers Stadium 1338

San Francisco 49ers at Pittsburgh Steelers

Monday Night Football has become a sports institution, and deservedly so; many of the NFL's best matchups are scheduled for Mondays; home teams often rise to a new level on Monday nights, and a festive atmosphere envelops every city when the Monday night show comes to town; I've gone to as many as eight of the Monday games in a single season; my first was in Pittsburgh; it was not a good 49er team that lost 27-0 to the Steelers that night; not the greatest game I've seen, but a pleasant night in one of America's most underrated and underappreciated sports cities; I always enjoy games in Pittsburgh, a great city with great sports fans.

Boston, April 17, 1978

GAME

1387  Fenway Park

Milwaukee Brewers at Boston Red Sox

GAME

1388 Boston Garden

Chicago Blackhawks at Boston Bruins

Patriots Day is celebrated only in Massachusetts, but it is always a special sports day in Boston; while the day is best known for the Boston Marathon, Patriots Day to me means the annual Red Sox mid-day baseball game. On this day, my eight year old son John was along for his first visit to Fenway; while looking for tickets, I decided to check at the box office, not a bad idea an hour or so before games since sometimes tickets held for VIPs are released for sale. The surly old ticket seller looked at me and said: "Sure I have two, buddy, they're the mayor's seats, he couldn't make it". I thought he was being sarcastic; he was telling the truth; we watched the Red Sox from the second row, right alongside the Red Sox dugout. Between games, we watched marathoners in various states of exhaustion stumbling through Back Bay; later, we headed to the Garden for a Stanley Cup playoff game between the Bruins and Hawks.

Long Island, April 29, 1978

GAME

1392 Nassau Coliseum

Toronto Maple Leafs at New York Islanders

I made my move for the parking lot on Lanny McDonald's backswing. I knew the puck was in the net for a sudden-death overtime Leafs victory over the favored Islanders in the seventh game of the playoff series. The Cinderella team of three years earlier was starting to disappoint the local fans, who now had unfulfilled visions of Stanley Cups; I cared little about the outcome; being there for the seventh and deciding game of any playoff series is good enough for me. John McCauley was to be the standby official that night, and sent over a couple of tickets so we could watch the game together; a few minutes into the game, a linesman was injured and McCauley had to take over in the unfamiliar role of linesman in the most important game of the season; he did well, but welcomed the news that, henceforth, for decisive playoff matches, two standby officials, one referee and one linesman, would be assigned, so that no one would have to officiate "out of position" again.

104 G 103

AISLE ROW SEAT

GAME

Atlanta Fulton County Stadium **1400**

Houston Astros at Atlanta Braves

My usual source of game tickets is the "curb exchange" a k a "the walk", a place near every venue where buyers and sellers negotiate transactions at prices that may differ significantly (upward or downward) from the "face" price on the ticket. Braves tickets are now a hot commodity, but such was not always the case. Certainly not when the Braves and Astros battled for last place in the final week of the 1978 season. I was approached by a well-dressed man asking if I would take his extra ticket, free of charge, providing I sit with him; he was unreasonably excited about the prospect of my joining him, but his ticket was in an excellent spot, right over the dugout, so I accepted; his joy was uncontrollable; when we got to the seats, he exclaimed "Pay up!" and collected $50 from his friends. They had bet he couldn't give away the ticket. But for my business trip to Atlanta, I think he would have lost the bet.

317 H 10

SEC. ROW SEAT

PROMENADE $5.00

NASSAU COLISEUM

GAME

Nassau Coliseum **1425**

Cincinnati Kids at New York Arrows

I have little use for indoor soccer (or for the other "imitation" sports such as Arena Football and Roller Hockey which lack any sense of connection to the tradition of the sport they mimic); how, for example, do you evaluate whether rushing for a hundred yards in Arena football is good or not? There are no standards, no history, no traditions, just the immediate spectacle. Eight year old boys love the action, so I brought my son and a friend to the Coliseum this night. If the Coliseum posted a sign: "No Adults Admitted Unless Accompanied by a Child" the crowd would have been no smaller. I'm among a minority of Americans who enjoys real outdoor soccer, as played in the Olympics, World Cup and the various pro leagues that have come and gone; but I could never get attached to the pinball version; that was strictly for kids.

Los Angeles, January 1, 1979

GAME

1431  The Forum

Colorado Rockies at Los Angeles Kings

SEAT   ROW   SEC

I vowed never again to travel on New Year's Day. Eager to get a fast start on a consulting engagement in Denver, I left home New Year's Day; I'd be in Denver two days, catch a Rockies game on the second, and be home for the weekend. But Denver Airport was closed by a snowstorm, expected to re-open late that night. I re-routed through Los Angeles and went to a game at the Forum. While at LAX a mild earthquake hit, shaking the terminal for several minutes and then subsiding. I got to Denver about 3am. Stranded skiers were everywhere, luggage strewn as far as the eye could see; people were crowding into the few available taxis. As we pulled away from the curb I saw a familiar figure, referee Wally Harris; he'd been marooned by the storm for days, missed an assignment in St. Louis and finally made it to Denver for the next night's game. I convinced my driver to stop and squeeze in one more passenger. We laughed about it the next night at Ebbets Field (the Denver pub named after the old Brooklyn ballpark) following the Rockies game, but it wasn't funny at the time on this unhappiest of New Years.

Quebec City, November 20, 1979

GAME

1491  Le Colisee

Boston Bruins at Quebec Nordiques

The NHL expanded again in 1979-80, absorbing four franchises from the defunct World Hockey Association. With twenty-one teams now in the league, I was nearing the limit of my ability to complete the circuit each year; but the four new cities seemed within my reach at least for this season. I'd been to Quebec City several times previously; in fact, I had seen Wayne Gretzky play there as a Pee Wee in 1974, when he was eleven years old; Quebec is a historic, charming city on one's first visit, and maybe the second. After that, it is unfriendly, small, unpleasant and fiercely Francofone. My high school and college French courses came in handy; the natives, for the most part, REFUSE to speak English; an Anglofone would have had a tough time negotiating a ticket to this game. I shed no tears when the Nordiques moved to Denver in 1995 to become the Colorado Avalanche.

Boston,   December 22, 1979

GAME

Boston Garden  **1502**

Philadelphia Flyers at Boston Bruins

Long Island,   December 22, 1979

GAME

Nassau Coliseum **1503**

Washington Capitals at New York Islanders

Year in and year out during the seventies, the Flyers and the Bruins gave hockey fans the most for their dollar. This Flyer team was on its way to a record thirty-five consecutive games without a loss; the streak stayed alive this Saturday afternoon in Boston. The old Garden on Causeway Street was my most frequent NHL haunt in the late seventies, both because of the appeal of the Bruins and a little known technique of airline ticket exchange that enabled me to shuttle to and from Boston for no more than ten dollars, usually less. If I had business in Chicago, for example, I'd buy the regular Chicago-New York ticket for business, then exchange it for a Chicago-Boston ticket, connecting on the Eastern shuttle, paying the additional fare myself; since I was working frequently in the West and Midwest I had an ample supply of New York-Boston coupons to get me to the best games. Two stops on the "T" from Logan, and I was at the Bruins front door. After the day game, I'd get the 4pm shuttle; there was more hockey in Long Island most Saturday nights.

New York,   December 23, 1979

GAME

Madison Square Garden **1504**

Boston Bruins at New York Rangers

They wear suits now, as an NHL general manager (Mike Milbury) and television commentator (Peter McNab), but on this night they were antagonists in a fiasco the video of which will live forever. Charging over the glass and fighting Rangers fans, this Bruin team not only beat the Rangers 4-3 but beat a Ranger fan over the head with his own shoe. It was comical; inexcusable, yes; certainly it never should have happened, but anyone who can't get a good laugh out of it is just too humorless to appreciate NHL hockey.

Edmonton, December 26, 1979

GAME

1505 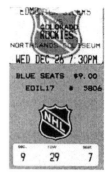 Northlands Coliseum

Colorado Rockies at Edmonton Oilers

Another Christmas week, another hockey trip, this one to Edmonton for my first visit there. I made it from New York with no difficulty, but the visiting Colorado Rockies were encountering serious airline problems enroute. For a while it even looked like the game would be postponed. I waited out the delay with the on-ice officials and some of the media; Rockies coach Don Cherry phoned from Spokane; they would take off momentarily and be in Edmonton an hour later. The game finally started at nine thirty; how foolish I would have felt if I'd flown all the way from New York to Edmonton for a game that wasn't played. But all's well that ends well; my flight out of Edmonton wasn't until 2am; by dawn, I was in Toronto, on much more familiar turf.

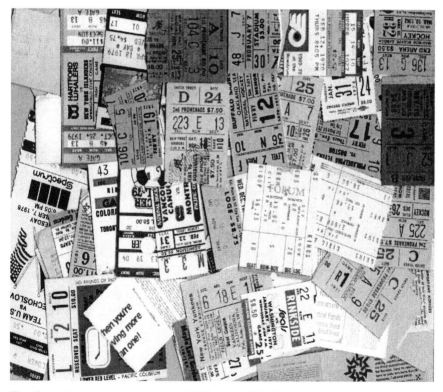

Chapter V

The 80's

Mixing Business With Pleasure

The eighties was a decade of dramatic change. My two children grew up and left for college. Their mother left for a new life and new husband; any my career took a new turn, as I transferred from New York to Minneapolis. Only the sports journey continued unaffected by life's transitions. I continued to travel to every NHL arena most seasons; as my son's youth sports years ended, my weekends were again available for NFL football. By the end of the decade, I was settled in Minnesota, but my work still took me to all corners of North America; by carefully coordinating my business and sport schedules, I added 704 games to my sports journey in the eighties, primarily hockey (402 games) and pro football (127); my games were distributed among twenty states, five provinces and the District of Columbia. I even attended part of the 1984 Olympics, and saw Australian Rules football in Melbourne.

Denver, March 20, 1980

GAME

McNichols Arena 1524

Quebec Nordiques at Colorado Rockies

When was a referee ejected from an NHL game? It sounds like a trick question, like the Trivial Pursuit question about who played for both the Brooklyn Dodgers and New York Rangers (organist Gladys Gooding). It isn't a trick question; of course Paul Stewart wasn't a referee in this game; later he became an NHL referee (and a good friend, who cooked Thanksgiving dinner for the crowd at my Minnesota home a few years back), but in 1979-80 he was the Quebec Nordiques "enforcer", a tough guy whose penalty minutes far exceeded his point totals. And as enforcers often do, he became embattled with a Colorado player, with the resulting fisticuffs earning him an ejection from referee Bryan Lewis. Sixteen years later referee Stewart presided at a Colorado Avalanche playoff game in the same building; Lewis was there as supervisor; it was his responsibility to inform Stewart that he had not been chosen to advance to the next round of the playoffs, ejecting him so to speak once again. Some things never change.

Long Island, May 17, 1980

GAME

Nassau Coliseum 1533

Philadelphia Flyers at New York Islanders

After falling short for several years, the Islanders are finally in the Stanley Cup finals, facing the Flyers; the Flyers dominated a regular season highlighted by their thirty-five game unbeaten streak; but in the playoffs, it is a different story; the Islanders win this game to take a two games to one lead in the series; they are a week away from the first of four consecutive Stanley Cups.

Long Island, May 24, 1980

I'm not at the Islander Stanley Cup finals game; I've offered to take my son John, an Islander fan for eight of his ten years, but he is first of all a player, not a spectator; it's only house league hockey, not one of the high pressure youth programs of the winter, but he'd rather play. I went to his rink with my portable television; John's favorite Islander, Bob Nystrom, scored the Cup winner in overtime. Was he sorry he hadn't gone to the game? No. Was I? No. The Stanley Cup is around forever. Children grow up too quickly; I think I had my priorities right.

Tampa, September 11, 1980

GAME

1550 Tampa Stadium

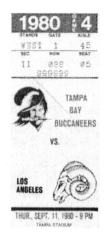

Los Angeles Rams
at Tampa Bay Buccaneers

I t's hard to remember, but the Tampa Bay Buccaneers were once sufficiently competitive to make an occasional national television appearance. It's a Thursday night ABC game against the Rams. I'm in Florida shopping for a condo; I pick up a ticket for half price and sit with the seller; turns out he's trying to unload a beachfront unit in Indian Rocks. Unfortunately, his condo price was not as negotiable as football ticket price. The next day I found a nice two bedroom waterfront condo in Treasure Island, which has been my second home, and headquarters for Florida sports travel, ever since.

Los Angeles, February 10, 1981

GAME

1581 The Forum

NHL All Star Game

A ll star games don't excite me, least of all the touch football spectacle called Pro Bowl and the NHL annual throw the goalies to the wolves shooting gallery. But business took me to Los Angeles so of course I went to the game. I'd rather watch any two NHL teams battle with intensity in a game that matters, but this night Campbell vs. Wales was the matchup du jour. (Even I was never totally sure which teams played in which conference; after all, I went to only seventy or eighty games a year). There are some very distant seats in the Forum, and while mine was far from the worst in the house, I wanted to be closer to the ice. I was near a refreshment stand at ice level when I realized my pale blue sport jacket was (except for missing the Hockey Night in Canada crest) identical to those worn by both English and French language Canadian television broadcasters, several of whom were stationed in the runway leading to the ice. I mingled with the group, figuring I'd go to my seat when my credentials (which of course I didn't have) were challenged; I watched the entire game without anyone saying a word to me; of course, sometimes clothing can work to your disadvantage. Once I made the mistake of wearing a red blazer and blue slacks to the Montreal Forum; I was asked by many fans to direct them to their seat before arriving at my own.

SEC.	ROW	SEAT
S	**19**	**41**

RESERVED SEAT $21.00

TUESDAY
7:30 P.M.
FEB. 17, 1981

CALGARY
vs.
ST. LOUIS
STAMPEDE CORRAL

GAME
Stampede Corral 🏒 1582
St. Louis Blues at Calgary Flames

The Atlanta Flames relocated to Calgary in the fall of 1980, so I had a new stop on my annual NHL tour; as the Saddledome was being built the Flames played for two years in a seven thousand seat building on the grounds of the Calgary Stampede; so hungry were Calgarians for hockey, season tickets were rationed; instead of getting a whole season, subscribers received their seats for only half the games, enabling more people to see NHL hockey, and giving the Flames potentially fourteen thousand season subscribers for the new building. In this atmosphere, I knew that it would be more challenging than usual to get myself a game ticket; arriving well before game time, I found several entrepreneurs with whom I could deal, for a price, a very high price. One of them, Peter, a sales rep by day, ticket broker by night urged me to be patient and the price would come down; he even tried to negotiate on my behalf with a fellow broker, a stern looking Indian whose ticket was excellent but asking price quite high. I tried my own luck; his piercing eyes looked directly into mine as he said: "Scalping, that's what my people are known for!" Further negotiation seemed inadvisable, so I paid his asking price and headed into the building. Peter was apologetic, and told me to call him next season and he'd take me to a Flames game as his guest; I assumed his business had season tickets. I enjoyed the Flames-Blues game in the intimate atmosphere of the tiny old Corral, got a post-game snack and headed for the airport, filing Peter's business card for possible future reference.

GAME
RFK Stadium ⚽ 1601
NewYork Cosmos at Washington Diplomats

For a few years the North American Soccer League gave respectability and a level of fan attention to pro soccer. Then the league disappeared as suddenly as it had grown in the late seventies; my view is that not enough Americans care to watch soccer, no matter how many may play the game. My attendance at the Cosmos-Diplomats game occurred solely because my eleven year old son was playing in a weekend tournament in Virginia; players and spectators are almost mutually exclusive groups, however. My son, now nearing age thirty, still plays and coaches soccer but as a spectator prefers the Dallas Cowboys, the New York Yankees and New York Islanders. While the North American Soccer League was around, I went to a couple of dozen games, mostly in Washington and New York, and really enjoyed the sport; but I think is just too alien to the American experience to ever achieve commercial success in this country.

Chicago, June 10, 1981

GAMES
1603, 1604 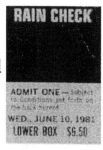 Wrigley Field
San Francisco Giants at Chicago Cubs

GAME
1605 Comiskey Park
New York Yankees at Chicago White Sox

It's amazing how many people I'd meet who, like myself, would seek out those days when the Cubs and White Sox were both home; two of baseball's best parks in the same city in the same day was quite a magnet for sports travelers. This day was even better; the Cubs completed a previously suspended game before their regular game with the Giants, so technically I saw three games in one Chicago day. Few Chicagoans would partake of this opportunity, since Cubs and Sox fans are mutually exclusive groups with great animosity toward one another. I marvel at how otherwise sensible baseball fans will refuse to go to the "other" Chicago ballpark, even though these two teams, in their long histories, have never played each other in a game that meant anything. It reminds me of my childhood when Dodger fans hated Giant fans and vice versa, but at least those teams competed head to head in the same league. In contrast, New York fans today are closer to bi-partisan than ever. Much of the same throng cheering the Yankees at their World Series victory parade last year would be there for a Mets parade as well. Such would not be the case in Chicago, although who knows how many more generations it may take for the Chicago ball clubs to put my theory to the test.

QUESTION FREQUENTLY ASKED OF THE AUTHOR:

Do You Play Any Sports Yourself?

I played some football and baseball in high school, and learned to skate well enough to play some midnight league hockey as an adult; until recently, I played tennis and softball; now I work with a personal trainer at my health club, and sometimes shoot hoops; no slam dunks; five foot five over fifty-five white guys not only can't jump, some days they can barely walk.

Philadelphia,   October 9, 1981

GAME

Veterans Stadium 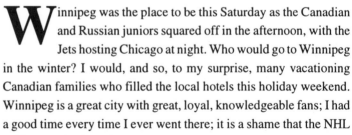 **1616**

Montreal Expos at Philadelphia Phillies

GAME

Spectrum **1617**

Detroit Red Wings at Philadelphia Flyers

In this oddest of baseball seasons, interrupted for seven weeks by a strike, an added round of playoffs preceded the usual League Championship Series. The Phillies and Expos battled at the Vet in a 4pm start. To paraphrase Ernie Banks, my motto might have been: "Let's watch two!" By itself the Phillies playoff might not have lured me down the Turnpike, but coupled with the Flyers and Red Wings opening night festivities, I was headed for my favorite street corner, Broad and Pattison, by early afternoon.

Winnipeg,   December 26, 1981

GAME

Winnipeg Arena **1633**

Soviet Juniors at Canada

GAME

Winnipeg Arena **1634**

Chicago Blackhawks at Winnipeg Jets

Winnipeg was the place to be this Saturday as the Canadian and Russian juniors squared off in the afternoon, with the Jets hosting Chicago at night. Who would go to Winnipeg in the winter? I would, and so, to my surprise, many vacationing Canadian families who filled the local hotels this holiday weekend. Winnipeg is a great city with great, loyal, knowledgeable fans; I had a good time every time I ever went there; it is a shame that the NHL simply outgrew this great hockey city.

Detroit, January 24, 1982

GAME

1640

Pontiac Silverdome

San Francisco 49ers
vs. Cincinnati Bengals

It was my first Super Bowl, and the first of many for the 49ers. My friend Jerry, from my Kezar days, didn't forget the original source of his now prized 49er season tickets; he was in New York on business, so we flew to Detroit together; at LaGuardia I ran into a local ticket broker on his way to the game; I told him I had my game tickets already; he said that was good because game tickets were really tough to come by this year, but told me he had "something even better". What could that be, we wondered. He flashed an envelope containing about fifty plane tickets. "I bought out the ten o'clock flight back to New York, and a snowstorm's coming to Detroit. Anyone wanting to get back tonight and beat the storm is going to have to deal with me!" Shrewd. We pick up our rental car and take the forty-seven mile drive to the Silverdome; EVERYTHING is for sale along Opdyke Road leading to the Dome, everything that is except parking. The stadium lots are completely reserved and no provision has been made for alternate lots; we found a lawn across from the Dome, gave the homeowner a thirty dollar donation to the Abbysynian Baptist Church and got to the game in plenty of time to enjoy the 49ers first Super Bowl victory. Back at the airport, we went our separate ways, Jerry to California, me to New York; as I headed to the departure gate I saw a familiar figure with an envelope: "Who needs tickets, who needs tickets?" The ten o'clock to New York was filling up fast.

GAME

Stampede Corral 1645

Washington Capitals at Calgary Flames

The Flames are still playing in the tiny Corral, so I'll call Peter's bluff and have him take me to the game. It turns out he doesn't exactly have season tickets, or any tickets for that matter; nevertheless he insists I allow him to take me to the game, free of charge, as his guest; we meet outside the Saddledome an hour before face off; a fair number of fans have extra tickets for sale, but Peter insists that I not buy any; he is approaching everyone coming to the game, basically begging for tickets; I am mortified. Game time is approaching; this is ridiculous; tickets are being offered for next to nothing, but not for absolutely nothing. Peter buys some more time; he told me he promised to take me to the game for free and he wants the chance to keep his promise. Shortly before game time, amazingly, someone hands Peter a pair of tickets, and we go to the game. Of all the ways I've gotten game tickets, this was definitely the most bizzare, and most embarrassing.

Long Island, May 14, 1983

GAME

Nassau Coliseum 1678

Edmonton Oilers at New York Islanders

The Islanders are a week away from their fourth consecutive Stanley Cup; their 5-1 victory will be the last game at the Coliseum this year as they will win the Cup in Edmonton; I'm directly behind the Edmonton bench, and have a video tape of the game telecast; the tape serves two purposes; it shows how age has caught up with me the last decade and also proves that I actually did go to Islander games despite how underimpressed I was with their arena; for the team's first eighteen seasons, I lived less than ten minutes away; I did attend 193 of their games, a lot of games, but a small percentage of the 728 they played; in only two of the seasons did I buy season tickets; the four-time Stanley Cup champions never really did capture the imagination of this hockey fanatic, despite being right in each other's back yard.

Foxboro, September 4, 1983

GAME

1688 Sullivan Stadium

Baltimore Colts at New England Patriots

It is the worst in pro sports; I would not insult any other stadium by declaring it second worst. Foxboro Stadium (previously known as Sullivan Stadium and Schaefer Stadium) would be an embarrassment to a medium-size Texas high school. Forty miles from nowhere, one narrow road leads to mud drenched parking lots; the stadium is convenient to nothing, except maybe Walpole State Prison; inmates on passes wouldn't go to Patriots games either; they wouldn't want to associate with the typical Patriots fan; what then brought me to this miserable spot? My son was playing hockey in Boston later that afternoon; I could either go to a sporting event or spend endless hours with other hockey parents agonizing over every second of ice time their son did, or did not, play. Given that choice, the Patriots, their stadium, and even their fans, looked pretty good.

Baltimore, September 11, 1983

GAME

1689 Memorial Stadium

Denver Broncos at Baltimore Colts

Memorial Stadium was not one of my favorites either; steamy and uncomfortable, with parking located at a high school a mile away, the Stadium offered little comfort, but lots of football and baseball nostalgia. The Broncos rookie quarterback John Elway had been drafted by the Colts but insisted on playing somewhere other than Baltimore; Elway's snub of their city fired the Colts fans to a greater frenzy than usual, an unnecessary increase in the already ample level of lunacy; Elway quieted the crowd with a 17-10 Denver victory; that winter, the Colts moving van headed for Indianapolis, and a glorious era suddenly, sadly ended. I much prefer the comfort of the RCA Dome to the Colts former home in Baltimore, but still don't like the way the Colts got to Indiana.

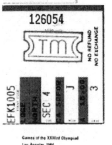

Los Angeles,   October 5, 1983

GAME

Dodger Stadium ⚾ **1690**

Philadelphia Phillies at Los Angeles Dodgers

GAME

The Forum 🏒 **1691**

Minnesota North Stars at Los Angeles Kings

More often than not I find the League Championship Series, leading up to the World Series, to be more exciting than the Series itself. Such was certainly the case in 1983 when two of my National League favorites squared off in the LCS; Fernando Valenzuela was the star of this game, hitting a home run and pitching the Dodgers to a 4-1 victory; eventually the Phillies prevailed and went on to the World Series, but this day belonged to the Dodgers and I was thrilled to be on hand in baseball's most beautiful setting. Thanks to television, lots of sporting events are played at odd times of day; the LCS started at 5pm, prime time on the East Coast; that enabled me to start my NHL hockey season later that day, arriving at the nearly deserted Forum before the North Stars and Kings had completed the first period.

Annapolis,   August 1, 1984

GAME

Navy-Marine Corps Stadium **1724**

Yugoslavia vs. Canada

My only Olympic event ever was a soccer match in the early rounds of 1984 competition; I'd be awfully unlikely to be found in the chaos of the principal Olympic venues, but this early round match was played not in Los Angeles but at Annapolis; I was working in Washington much of this summer so it was an easy drive to the game on a pleasant evening. Without really thinking about it, I expected the kind of all-Canadian, pro-Canadian crowd that an international hockey match might have attracted. How wrong I was. I should never underestimate the amount of national pride at stake when European nations participate in world soccer competition; the crowd was overwhelmingly pro-Yuogoslav; it was not only a great way to experience the Olympics without going to Los Angeles, it was a great way to experience a foreign environment without any need for a passport or plane ticket.

Scottsdale, April 2, 1985

GAME

1763  Scottsdale Stadium

Seattle Mariners at San Francisco Giants

Phoenix, April 2, 1985

GAME

1764 Phoenix Municipal Stadium

Cleveland Indians at Oakland Athletics

A morning meeting and a late afternoon flight was a combination that enabled me to get to my first two Arizona spring training games. After three innings at Scottsdale, I went to Phoenix, arriving in the fourth inning. As I walked toward the stadium from my car, a foul ball came over the stands and rolled right to me. Not exactly a spectacular catch in the stands, but the foul ball was all mine. My first foul ball was far gentler than Jim Brennan's first hockey puck.

Los Angeles, May 30, 1985

GAME

1774 L.A. Memorial Coliseum

Denver Gold at Los Angeles Express

GAME

1775  Dodger Stadium

Philadelphia Phillies at Los Angeles Dodgers

L os Angeles is known for its late arriving sports crowds. Crowds for the World Football League Express arrived too late to save the franchise, even though the team was led by a legitimate franchise player, quarterback Steve Young. The 6pm kickoff at the Coliseum allowed me to stay for a half, get on the freeway and join the late arriving, but much larger, crowd at Dodger Stadium.

ENTER GATE 9
GAME **5**
SEC. ROW SEAT
109 6 7
SUNDAY SEPT. 29, 1985
12:00 Noon SOLDIER FIELD
TICKET PRICE $14.00
STADIUM SERV CHGE 1.00
TOTAL PRICE $15.00

GAME

Soldier Field  **1781**

Washington Redskins at Chicago Bears

GAME

Wrigley Field **1782**

Philadelphia Phillies at Chicago Cubs

GAME

Chicago Stadium **1783**

Edmonton Oilers at Chicago Blackhawks

Enter Gate 1
4 D B 13
AISLE SEC. ROW SEAT
FIRST BALCONY
NO REFUNDS OR EXCHANGES $10.00

BLACKHAWKS vs. EDMONTON OILERS

SUNDAY 7:30 P.M.
SEPT. 29, 1985

Sports travel heaven; three games, three sports, all in one day in America's most enjoyable big city. I picked up a Cubs ticket in the morning and then headed for the Bears game. A cab ride to Wrigley got me to the last six innings of the Phillies-Cubs game. Lots of time left for a good dinner and a night at the world's greatest hockey arena. It was only a pre-season Blackhawks game, but still a great day. All three Chicago teams won, which means nothing to me, but was probably of some significance in a city which takes all its own teams quite seriously.

#78
CHICAGO CUBS VS.
PHILADELPHIA
WRIGLEY FIELD
SUN 1:20 PM
SEP 29 1985

ENTER GATE 26
GAME **6**
SEC. ROW SEAT
126 3 16
MONDAY OCT. 21, 1985
9:00 P.M. SOLDIER FIELD
TICKET PRICE $14.00
STADIUM SERV CHGE 1.00
TOTAL PRICE $15.00

Jim Taylor

BEARS VS.

GAME

Soldier Field  **1787**

Green Bay Packers at Chicago Bears

Monday Night Football, the Packers and Bears; the NFL gets no better than this. This game will be remembered as the one in which coach Mike Ditka turned William "The Refrigerator" Perry into a running back, and he blasted through for short yardage for a late touchdown to solidify a win over the hated Packers.

Washington, November 18, 1985

GAME

1797 R F K Stadium

New York Giants at Washington Redskins

I had Redskins tickets for years but never occupied my own season seats until now. Business associates conspired to keep me from learning how good the seats were, for fear I would start to show up regularly. I did start showing up now and then, but no Skins game had the drama, and tragedy, of this one. Quarterback Joe Theismann suffered a career ending broken leg; backup Jay Schroeder led the Redskins to a dramatic 23-21 victory, but the Theismann injury dampened everyone's spirits at RFK that night.

Miami, December 2, 1985

GAME

1800 Orange Bowl

Chicago Bears at Miami Dolphins

I t was the best ever season for the Chicago Bears; they seemed on the way to matching the 1972 Dolphins' unbeaten march through the Super Bowl. The biggest obstacle in the Bears way was the 1985 Dolphins; before the most excited, hysterical crowd in the long history of dramatic Orange Bowl games, both pro and college, the Dolphins prevailed 38-24 for the Bears only defeat of the season. Miami looked forward to beating the Bears a second time in the Super Bowl seven weeks later, but their path to the big game was still, despite this great victory, a difficult one, as the AFC race was perhaps the most competitive ever during this 1985 season.

GAME

Orange Bowl **1807**

New England Patriots at Miami Dolphins

T here is a thin line between being enjoyably decadent and totally disgusting. The Orange Bowl crowd walked that line regularly; back in the Orange Bowl for another Monday night I went to my seat early, to avoid the human crush in the narrow tunnel leading to the main seating area. The partying had begun hours before game time; in fact, some of the partiers were in very bad shape by an hour BEFORE kickoff; one was stretched out, semi-conscious, in the row in front of my season ticket location. Closer inspection revealed this individual's previously-eaten dinner spread across several seats in row fourteen; surely those seats would be occupied, and the ticket holders should be warned lest they sit down without looking; all of the early arrivals noticed the hazard and were on the lookout for the ticketholders. Suddenly, a group of about six fans, dressed head to toe in Patriot colors, headed directly for row fourteen. No one offered one word of warning.

New York, December 22, 1985

GAME

Giants Stadium **1808**

Pittsburgh Steelers at New York Giants

GAME

Nassau Coliseum **1809**

New York Rangers at New York Islanders

G iants Stadium is the finest NFL stadium. Not only is the design perfect for watching football, the Giants following is (save for meaningless games where many tickets are sold by the original owners) among the most civilized in sports. Giant tickets have been passed through generations and a high proportion of regular Giant fans have been attending the games for decades, starting at a time when the world was less tolerant of the outrageous behavior of some of the younger fans. When the Jets moved from Shea Stadium to Giants Stadium in 1983, a similar upgrading of fan behavior seemed to occur almost immediately. I never quite understood why; the Jets fans I knew were every bit as out of control as they had been at Shea. I sat at this Giant game with an older man who explained succinctly, but perceptively, the behavioral phenomenon: "You can get to Shea Stadium on the city subway, but not to Giants Stadium." Enough said. Later that day, watching some of the Ranger faithful following their team on the road, I feared that the subway line had, during the day, been extended into Nassau County; Rangers-Islanders games tend to bring out the lowest element of each team's constituency.

New York,   December 22, 1985

GAME

1810  Giants Stadium

Cleveland Browns at New York Jets

GAME

1811 Byrne Meadowlands Arena

Minnesota North Stars at New Jersey Devils

T he Jet Pack is a group of business owners, professionals, assorted gypsies, tramps and thieves of various origin and occupation, who are unified by a common, unwavering loyalty to Jets football. They all recall their whereabouts when time began: that glorious day of January 12, 1969 when the Jets toppled the heavily favored Baltimore Colts in Super Bowl III. The hard core Jet Packers were at that game, as well as at virtually every Super Bowl since. My good friend Richie is the acknowledged "leader of the pack"; his Jets home game attendance streak goes back to the New York Titans at the Polo Grounds in 1962; an Elvis lookalike who could win a Fifties Costume contest without changing clothes, he supervises the tailgating needs of up to fifteen hundred hungry Jets fans before each game, and re-opens the tailgate for a couple of hours following each home game. The whole Jet Pack experience goes on the road for about half the Jets away games each year, motivated by the need to keep in top partying shape for the upcoming Super Bowl. This year, for the second time in three years, the Jets look like they might actually have a chance to get to the Super Bowl, so the Jet Pack post-game festivities last until well after dark; I actually had to leave early just to cross the parking lot to the Devils game.

SEC. ROW SEAT
123   9   4

Ticket Price   22.00
Stadium Serv. Chge   1.00
Total Price   23.00

NO REFUND OR EXCHANGE

NFC Playoff

Enter Gate 4

11 K A 28
AISLE SEC. ROW SEAT

FIRST BALCONY
NO REFUNDS
OR EXCHANGES $10.00

BLACKHAWKS
vs.
MINNESOTA
NORTH STARS

SUNDAY 7:30 PM.
JAN. 5, 1986

LES NORDIQUES #22.00
reçoivent au Colisée de Québec
LOS ANGELES
18 FEVRIER 1986
Mardi à 19H35
LODGE SECTION 21
13
527A 443 34

Chicago, January 5, 1986

GAME

Soldier Field 🏈 **1815**

New York Giants at Chicago Bears

GAME

Chicago Stadium 🏒 **1816**

Minnesota North Stars at Chicago Blackhawks

It was my coldest sporting event. A day earlier, I was sweltering in the Orange Bowl sun at the Dolphins play-off game, but had fortunately packed warm clothing for my weekend football trip. Heaters beneath the stands at Soldier Field were surrounded by fans trying to get some warmth during commercial breaks. Normally I'm not really troubled by temperatures, high or low, but this day was exceptional; certainly the weather had something to do with Giants punter Sean Landetta actually missing the ball while attempting to punt; the Giants were probably no match for the Bears this year in any stadium or any weather; the Bears march to the Super Bowl continued with a 21-0 shutout. As usual after a Bears home game, traffic moved erratically on the Chicago streets and the Blackhawks crowd was even more boisterous than ever. Lots of anti-freeze was consumed at Soldier Field on cold Sundays.

Quebec City, February 18, 1986

GAME

Le Colisse 🏒 **1826**

Los Angeles Kings at Quebec Nordiques

My children, when teenagers, always had a school vacation week in February; each year we would take a sports trip for a few days; this year's stops were in Montreal and Quebec City; my son was fluent in languages, having won the school awards in both French and Spanish, the academic equivalent of the Stanley Cup and Olympic Gold in the same year. What a surprise when he could not understand a word of the Quebec dialect, and showed even less interest in attempting to understand the natives. Fortunately, my French was more Quebecois than Parisian, so I could negotiate for game tickets, taxis and meals; we thoroughly enjoyed the NHL games in Montreal and Quebec, if little else; our future February trips would be to Southern California.

New York,   September 21, 1986

GAME

1858 Giants Stadium

Miami Dolphins at New York Jets

hose who make a silly issue of the NEW YORK Giants and Jets playing their home games in New Jersey should focus instead on the teams' good fortune in playing home games in the NFL's finest stadium (which is of course well within the New York City metro area). As for the added trouble of traveling to New Jersey from Long Island, I personally discredited that concern when this Dolphins-Jets thriller ended with a 51-45 Jets victory, on an overtime touchdown pass from Ken O'Brien to Wesley Walker. I snapped a photo of the game winner, at 4pm, and dashed to the parking lot. Ron's photo shop in Long Island closes at five on Sundays, but my photo of the game winner was ready by closing.

Boston,   October 7, 1986

GAME

1861 Fenway Park

California Angels at Boston Red Sox

nly the Angels stand between the Red Sox and the World Series. Finally the "Curse of the Bambino" that has, as the story goes, doomed the Red Sox to perpetual post-season failure since they traded Babe Ruth to the Yankees, may be over! But to the Sox chagrin, the Angels (naturally without the benefit of any visiting partisans in attendance at Fenway) prevail 8-1 in the opener of the best of five League Championship Series. I was on hand the next afternoon as well, when the Sox evened the LCS at a game apiece; over the weekend they got two more victories in Anaheim, setting the stage for the classic 1986 Mets-Red Sox showdown.

Boston, October 21, 1986

GAME

Fenway Park 1865

New York Mets at Boston Red Sox

My college friend Mike was a life long Red Sox fan; we were scheduled to meet for dinner; I knew his purpose was to solicit a substantial donation for the Williams twenty-fifth anniversary alumni endowment fund. I suggested we eat early and try to go to the World Series game. Mike told me I'd never get tickets, thereby confirming that we had not been that close since graduation. I arrive at our Newbury Street steak house a few minutes late for our 6pm reservation, but carrying two "Upper Box" (which as the name does not suggest, are actually excellent lower deck seats at Fenway) seats behind first base. Mike knew these tickets were trading at a hefty price and asked, warily: "How much do I owe you for the ticket?" My reply: "One percent of whatever outrageous amount you're about to ask me to donate to the college." The subject turned to baseball in a hurry; I settled for all the cash Mike had on him, generously bought a sweatshirt for him to take home to his young son, and threw in a "T" token, so he could take the subway back to where his car was parked following the game. Negotiation becomes second nature as it is practiced so frequently during sports travel.

Pasadena, January 25, 1987

GAME

1904 Rose Bowl

Denver Broncos vs. New York Giants

It's my first Super Bowl as a member of the "hard core" of the Jet Pack. I'm appointed chief navigator and am driving the lead car of a caravan in search of the Rose Bowl. Game time is some six hours away, but its never too early to tailgate on such a beautiful day. I had only a vague idea of how to get to the Rose Bowl; following what I thought to be a road, I inadvertently turned across the lawn of a church where parishioners were filing in for services. People began waving frantically at me to stop; pretending not to see, I crossed the lawn heading for the road I knew we wanted to get to; the entire caravan followed, a parade of cars and vans displaying Jets insignia leaving bewildered parishioners in this small town to scatter in a hurry. Finally, we got close to the Rose Bowl, or as close as one could, given that heavy rains had closed the main parking lot. Somewhere in Southern California, within a couple mile walk of the stadium, the Jet Pack party began in earnest. Yes, there was a football game. The Giants beat the Broncos; for the most part, we were quite pleased. After all, the Jet Pack consists almost entirely of native New Yorkers and Jet fans are descended from Giant fans. Only Richie has the contrarian view; he's an AFC guy all the way, so he suffered with the Broncos; John Elway and his "Three Amigos" receiving corps were no match for the Giants this day, but would get another chance at a Super Bowl ring a year later. The Jet Pack was already making plans for 1988 in San Diego.

Los Angeles, February 14, 1987

GAME

1912  The Forum

New York Express at Los Angeles Lazers

GAME

1913 The Forum

Hartford Whalers at Los Angeles Kings

February break found my children and me in Southern California. Whatever the event, we were there. The NHL Kings were the top attraction but we'd seek out all the events we could find; an afternoon of indoor soccer reminded me that the choice of events was not mine alone. Fortunately, I was accompanied by children, so I was permitted to buy a ticket for the Lazers game.

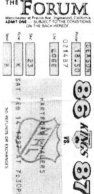

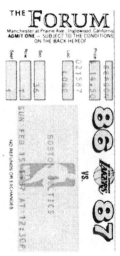

GAME

The Forum 1914

Boston Celtics at Los Angeles Lakers

In the eighties, nothing beat the Celtics-Lakers, Bird vs Magic matchup. The stars are out, courtside, and scattered throughout the crowd. Magic's buzzer beating three pointer gives the Lakers the last second 106-103 victory; after the game we witness a minor scuffle in the parking lot; my son recognizes an actor from a police series; for a moment we expect him to move in and make an arrest; only then do we get it, this is real life, the other is television; sometimes it's tough to tell the difference in LA.

San Francisco, July 26, 1987

GAMES

Candlestick Park 1949, 1950

St. Louis Cardinals (doubleheader) at San Francisco Giants

The endangered, nearly extinct, tradition lives one more day; the regularly scheduled Sunday doubleheader, Cardinals and Giants; uniforms that look very similar to what I saw at the Polo Grounds in 1948; a beautiful day at Candlestick, bright sun and no wind. Baseball grows on you; the first inning can be boring, by the fifth it is interesting, and it keeps getting better and better; I stayed for all nineteen innings, a ten inning Cardinal first game victory, and a 5-2 Giants win in the nightcap.

San Diego, January 31, 1988

GAME

1987 San Diego-
Jack Murphy Stadium
Denver Broncos
vs. Washington Redskins

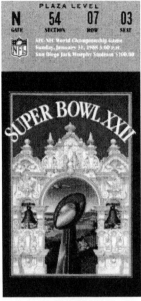

The Jet Pack doesn't have a lot of rules; this politically incorrect, but kindhearted band of zealots have only one tribal taboo: NO WOMEN AT SUPER BOWL! (at least not one whose acquaintance was made more than, say, thirty-six hours prior to kickoff). It was my biggest blunder. No matter that I'd gotten two game tickets from the Redskins, and that no male member of the Jet Pack was in need of a game ticket. I was on "thin water", as my date put it. Jet Pack Probation, all brought about by the baby girl who first saw the light of day in Wisconsin as I was completing my baseball scorebook at the Polo Grounds so many years ago. Of course, it didn't help matters when at the post-game tailgate, the Jet Pack's unwelcome intruder, fueled by a bottle of sambuka pilfered from the official Jet Pack liquor cabinet, taunted the defeated, departing orange-clad Bronco fans with repeated toasts of:"Adios Amigos!" I would really need to pull off a miracle to restore my good Jet Pack standing before the next Super Bowl.

Toronto, March 5, 1988

GAME

1999 Maple Leaf Gardens
Winnipeg Jets at Toronto Maple Leafs

I celebrated my two thousandth game with my daughter Mary Beth during a hockey weekend in Canada; at Maple Leaf Gardens on Saturday night, before a national audience watching my favorite television series - Hockey Night in Canada - the Leafs were humiliated in one of their worst ever defeats at the Gardens, a 10-1 rout by the Winnipeg Jets.
Mary Beth enjoyed her first visit to Toronto, but was even more interested in our next game; an early Sunday morning flight took us to see her favorite team, the Islanders, in a matinee game at Quebec City to mark my two thousandth lifetime game.

GAME

Winnipeg Arena 🏒 2001

Edmonton Oilers at Winnipeg Jets

The London Hockey Nuts are like the Jet Pack in some ways, very different in others. All British, they include journalists, accountants, and assorted other professions in their membership. They have a keen interest in NHL hockey and make at least one, sometimes two, trips to North America each season, hopping from one city to the next to catch ten or more games on a fortnight's excursion. I first met the Nuts quite by chance as they sat directly behind me at a game some years earlier; I was impressed by the depth of their understanding of the game; they were more knowledgeable than probably eighty per cent of North American fans, despite their limited access to current NHL stats and information. (That percentage is now closer to ninety-nine, not because the Nuts know more, but because so many fans who know nothing have turned their interest, and their checkbooks, toward the NHL recently). I joined the Nuts for a delightful evening in Winnipeg; the Oilers, a dynasty on its way to another Stanley Cup, shut out the Jets 6-0; using comparative scores, I guess that made the Oilers fifteen goals superior to the Leafs this week.

Vancouver,   April 1, 1988

GAME

Pacific Coliseum 🏒 2007

Minnesota North Stars at Vancouver Canucks

The increasing difficulty of my irrational pursuit of one home game in each of the NHL's twenty-one cities produced some strange travel connections on the final weekend of several seasons. Going into the final weekend I still had four of the Canadian arenas to hit; the weekend started with a flight to the West Coast. The North Stars were playing out the schedule, and showed few signs of life in a 6-1 Canucks win; I'd catch up with the Stars before the weekend was over, but following the game I was off to Vancouver airport for a red-eye to the East.

Montreal, April 2, 1988

GAME

2008  Olympic Stadium

New York Yankees at Montreal Expos

GAME

2009 Montreal Forum

Buffalo Sabres at Montreal Canadiens

The red-eye got to Montreal in time for an added bonus to my hockey trip, a spring training exhibition game. My first and only visit to Olympic Stadium matched the Yankees with the Expos in the final weekend of exhibitions before regular season play began. The stadium is, with the possible exception of the Metrodome, the least appealing in major league baseball; the Olympic track separates the spectators from the game by a great distance; the Forum was, as ever, a thrilling venue, but it was off to bed early; my flight leaves at the crack of dawn.

Calgary, April 3, 1988

GAME

2010 Olympic Saddledome

Minnesota North Stars at Calgary Flames

Edmonton, April 3, 1988

GAME

2011 Northlands Coliseum

Los Angeles Kings at Edmonton Oilers

My Montreal to Calgary flight made an intermediate stop in Toronto; to my surprise, on came John Mc Cauley, spending his Easter Sunday afternoon supervising the officials in Calgary; we chatted throughout the flight, as we had done many times over the years; sadly, this would be the last time I would spend any time with John before his untimely death from complications of minor surgery. I was offered a ride back to the airport following the Calgary game, but declined; I couldn't wait around for the officials to leave since I had to catch a flight to Edmonton and head right to the Coliseum for a 6pm game; it would certainly be foolish to miss the one and only NHL arena I'd not been to this year on the season's final night.

New York,   April 12, 1988

GAME

Nassau Coliseum **2012**

New Jersey Devils at New York Islanders

My daughter Mary Beth and the Islanders were both born in Long Island in the summer of 1972. So I can not only excuse her Islander partisanship, I helped her indulge it by buying her Islander season tickets when she was in high school; she was right behind the goal so I could tune in on satellite and be sure she was at the game. Of course, for the big games, her second ticket belonged to Dad. Such was the case as the Islanders played the deciding game of the opening playoff round against the Devils at the Coliseum. The Devils eliminated the Islanders; Mary Beth, to her credit, did not let the defeat demoralize her; the next day she bought a Devils sweater (a "new New Jersey jersey", as she referred to it) and adopted the Devils as her team for the balance of the playoffs.

Washington,   April 30, 1988

GAME

Capital Centre **2014**

New Jersey Devils at Washington Capitals

The Devils and Capitals have gone to a seventh and deciding game, winner faces the Boston Bruins in the Stanley Cup semi-finals, loser goes home for the summer; my daughter turned Devil-worshipper and I are in Washington for the weekend; the Devils upset the favored Caps in a 3-2 thriller; we had such a good time that I suggested (never thinking this bluff would be called) that if the upcoming Bruins series extended to seven games, we should go to Boston the weekend after next for another Devils game seven.

New Jersey, May 8, 1988

GAME

2016 Byrne Meadowlands Arena
Boston Bruins at New Jersey Devils

The Devils-Bruins series was unique in that game 4 was officiated by replacement officials; John Mc Cauley sat at ice level to "coach" the replacements as best he could; anyone who minimizes the importance of NHL on-ice officials should watch a tape of this game; the replacements knew the game and were competent amateur hockey referees and linesmen; but they were as out of place as high school all-stars would have been in Devils or Bruins sweaters. A world class referee has a "feel" for the game enabling him to make the correct split-second judgments regulating the flow of the game to assure a fair outcome and minimal impact of illegal acts. Blow the whistle too often and the game becomes a travesty; overlook too much, and the game gets completely out of hand; say the wrong thing and intensify ill feeling; say the right thing to players and coaches and their focus will stay on the game; refereeing hockey is an art, and the best artists are wearing NHL striped shirts; fortunately, this game's outcome, a 3-1 Devils victory, was not too badly tainted; the Devils deserved to win. It is sometimes said that no one buys a ticket to watch the officials; this may be true, but in the absence of top game officials, it would not be worth buying tickets to watch the players; the NHL, with the help of "coach" Mc Cauley, dodged a huge bullet this night.

Boston, May 14, 1988

GAME

2018 Boston Garden
New Jersey Devils at Boston Bruins

Sure enough, the Devils-Bruins series went to a seventh game. Mary Beth and I checked into our hotel; she's proudly wearing her Devils attire and asks, jokingly, if room 666 has been pre-assigned to us. It's just a short walk from the hotel at Long Wharf to the Boston Garden. But the walk seems a lot longer when wearing the visitor's colors. (Personally, I never wear any partisan clothing to a game, but my family and friends don't always heed my advice). To say the least, Bruins fans were less hospitable to the New Jersey visitor than their Washington counterparts had been two weeks previously. As it turned out, the same was true for the Bruins team, as they easily eliminated the Devils by a 6-2 score. The Devils were home for the summer, and Mary Beth's jersey buried deep in her closet. My daughter the Devil-worshipper was once again an Islanders fan.

GAME

Wrigley Field  **2029**

New York Mets at Chicago Cubs

I probably qualify as a "purist", one who enjoys his sports as they were traditionally played; as such, I should have objected to the installation of lights at Wrigley Field, but for some strange reason, I did not. Much as I enjoy afternoon games at Wrigley, I didn't mind the idea of Cubs night games. Thirty seven years to the day after a rainout gave me a doubleheader in my first visit to Fenway, a rainout at Wrigley postponed the first night game so that it coincided with the date of a business commitment in Chicago. While tickets were trading north of $100 on Addison Street, I approached a neglected ticket window; sure enough, a single, twelve rows up, directly behind home plate was just added to the computer inventory. It never hurts to ask.

Minneapolis,   December 19, 1988

GAME

Metrodome **2082**

Chicago Bears at Minnesota Vikings

I've attended 195 games there, more than at any other baseball-football stadium. Yet relatively few of the Twins and Vikings games, much as I enjoy them, are that memorable. The Vikings never sell out the Metrodome. (Sold out games are attributable to the visiting Packers, Bears and other marquee teams). But this Monday Night Football match with the Bears was one to be remembered Mike Ditka's Bears, headed for the playoffs, have the game under control in the fourth quarter. Walker Lee Ashley's interception return for a touchdown gives the Vikings a dramatic 28-27 victory. Last minute Viking heroics against the Bears or Packers tend to be remembered forever, even by non-native Minnesotans such as myself.

Chicago, December 31, 1988

GAME

2087 Soldier Field

Phildelphia Eagles at Chicago Bears

GAME

2088 Metropolitan Sports Center

St. Louis Blues at Minnesota North Stars

I t will forever be remembered as the Fog Bowl. Late in the first half at Soldier Field a dense fog so covered the field that even in the fifteenth row from the sideline, I could not see a thing. The players could see barely well enough to allow the game to continue, but not well enough for the Eagles to mount any kind of attack once the fog hit; I left the game at halftime; why stay if you can't see anything. I was just hopeful my flight wouldn't be fogged in; but a mile west of the lake the day was clear and sunny. I was home in plenty of time for the traditional New Year's Eve North Stars hockey game at the Met.

My children's annual winter sports trip to Southern California

GAME

Joe Robbie Stadium 2098

Cincinnati Bengals
vs. San Francisco 49ers

Redemption time. Super Bowl XXIII. How do I get back in the good graces of the Jet Pack? Fate was on my side; I came up with two of the best seats in JRS, seven rows from the field, just where I like to sit, and on the thirty-five yard line, which will impress Richie, a card carrying yard-line guy who denominates the value of tickets solely by their proximity to the fifty. My locations are better than any in this year's Jet Pack inventory. I invite Richie to sit with me. Furthermore, I refuse to accept any money for the ticket. Bingo! I'm forgiven faster than Ford pardoned Nixon. Of course I remind Richie that my gesture does solidify in perpetuity my claim on Jets tickets any time I fly in for a home game. Since Richie controls over fifty season tickets, and the Jets no-show count exceeds the population of half the states in the Union, that will not be a difficult promise for him to keep. Restored to my role as navigator, I drive the lead car in the caravan to JRS. Elvis is alongside, holding all the game tickets. As we proceed at a crawl toward the JRS parking entrance, my rental car begins to overheat, smoke escaping from under the hood; we see a sign stating that vehicles will be admitted to the lot only if occupants show game tickets; thus, Richie needs to distribute tickets to the Jet Packers in vehicles following my overheating car. He bolts from the car and races back in the line of traffic, clutching a fistful of Super Bowl tickets. Seeing this panic evacuation of my overheating car, drivers on all sides assume an explosion is imminent and clear the way for our whole caravan to sail through traffic and on to the Stadium lot. One of the Jet Pack solved my radiator problem, probably leaving us short a couple of Coors in the process. But my troubles were not over. Biting into a piece of chicken at the tailgate party, one of my front teeth broke completely off; fortunately it was more ugly than painful, but I needed to set up emergency dental work. Phone booths were loaded with customers, far more of them calling bookmakers than dentists, but finally I got through and set up repairs for the next day back in Minnesota. So, net of my front tooth, I settled in for what, to that time, was the best football game I've ever seen. Joe Montana led the Niners to a come from behind fourth quarter victory; noticing the crowd it seemed that everyone over age forty was a 49er fan, tastefully dressed in red and tan; those under forty were predominately Bengal fans, and generally gross and ill behaved. Only one exception, my man Richie. He's well over forty, but he's an AFC guy all the way. When the post game tailgate broke up and I left for my hotel, Richie was still going strong; when last seen he was doing the Ickey Shuffle with a bimbo in Bengal gear whose only dental defect was a chipped tooth sustained while catching a frisbee.

Calgary, May 31, 1989

GAME

2125  Olympic Saddledome

Winnipeg Jets at Calgary Flames

After this last weekend trip filling in NHL arenas missed earlier in the season, I gave up trying to attend a game in each arena each year. My Friday flight to Calgary made an intermediate stop in Regina, the only time I've ever set foot in the province of Saskatchewan. The game was memorable for the first appearance of a player from the Soviet Union, Sergei Priakin, in an NHL game; there are so many Russians in the NHL now that one can easily forget how recently the first one appeared in the NHL. I had no time to reflect upon this memorable event as I had a red-eye out of Calgary to Toronto, with connections to Montreal and Quebec City.

Quebec, April 1, 1989

GAME

2126  Le Colisee

Boston Bruins at Quebec Nordiques

Long Island, April 1, 1989

GAME

2127  Nassau Coliseum

Buffalo Sabres at New York Islanders

I went to the Bruins-Quebec matinee for one reason only; Quebec was the one and only NHL arena where I had not attended a regular season game in 1988-89; fortunately, I stayed awake all day and caught a bit of a nap on late afternoon flights to Montreal and LaGuardia; I arrived in New York just about game time for the Islanders at the Nassau Coliseum; a fifty dollar cab ride and half a period later I joined Mary Beth at the Coliseum for the end of the 1988-89 regular season.

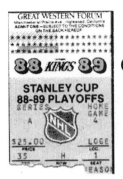

Los Angeles, April 15, 1989

GAME

Great Western Forum 2133
Edmonton Oilers at Los Angeles Kings

The Kings have given me many enjoyable evenings since their arrival in the NHL in the 1967 expansion; the Great Western Forum may not be the "Fabulous Forum" that original Kings owner Jack Kent Cooke preferred to hear it called, but it is a comfortable, very familiar stop on my NHL rounds each year. The natives viewed the Kings with conspicuous indifference for their first twenty-two seasons. But this year, Wayne Gretzky arrived and suddenly hockey is the sport du jour in Southern California. Gretzky's Kings are matched with his former team, the defending Cup champion Edmonton Oilers; the series goes to a seventh game; this one game is getting more attention in Los Angeles than the Kings used to attract in an entire season. Mary Beth and I flew out to Los Angeles Saturday morning for this "can't miss" game; the trip was well worth it; the Kings won 6-2; at the same time, Calgary and Vancouver also played a classic game seven, so I was glad I was video taping Hockey Night in Canada at home; we could have been back in Minnesota by dawn, but, thoughtful father that I am, I insisted Mary Beth have her first Dodger Stadium visit the next afternoon.

Boston, July 29, 1989

GAME

Nickerson Field 2143
Albany Capitols at Boston Bolts

Mary Beth and I are visiting colleges in the Boston area. The Red Sox are on the road, so as far as she is concerned, there are no games to attend. I convince her she wants to go to Nickerson Field (which she has never heard of) to watch a game in the American Soccer League (which she also has never heard of). Surely there has been some mistake. Call 911! My Dad has completely lost it! He's talking about trolley tracks entering the park on Gaffney Street, and pointing out where the right field pavilion and giant scoreboard used to be. Of course, my interest was not in the soccer game, but in revisiting the remnants of old Braves Field, the home of Boston's National League baseball team until they moved to Milwaukee in 1953. Mary Beth had better find a college where she can major in sports history if she wants to keep up with her Dad.

Atlanta, September 26, 1989

GAME

2159  The Omni

Philadelphia Flyers vs. Boston Bruins

A tlanta was in the NHL for eight seasons, 1972 through 1980, and The Omni was one of my favorite arenas; I was pleased, therefore, when two Boston Bruins pre-season games were set for Atlanta in the fall of 1989 and one coincided with a business trip. Despite the fact that the Flames had good attendance in their Atlanta years, I felt the general public in Atlanta never really caught on to hockey. Two well dressed businessmen were discussing the upcoming game just before the anthem. One asked the other: How do they decide who gets the puck first, do they flip a coin? The sad thing is, when the NHL returns to Atlanta, these guys will probably own a luxury suite.

Philadelphia, December 31, 1989

GAME

2209 Veterans Stadium

Los Angeles Rams at Philadelphia Eagles

Minneapolis, December 31, 1989

GAME

2210 Metropolitan Sports Center

St. Louis Blues at Minnesota North Stars

A nother New Year's Eve and more hard times for the Eagles; this time in the rain instead of the fog, and at home instead of on the road, the Eagles make another early exit from the NFL post season, as the Rams win a 21-7 yawner in the rain at the Vet. Fortunately, the 5pm to Minneapolis ran on time; I'll be home for the end of the decade of the eighties, but not until I've stopped enroute from the airport for the traditional Minnesota North Stars NHL New Year's Eve game at Met Center.

Chapter VI

The 90's

Retirement And Beyond

I opted for early retirement as soon as I turned age fifty, late in 1990, leaving the consulting rat race behind for a while; I really got serious about sports travel, adding 215 games to my journey in the next eighteen months, including forty-three Stanley Cup playoff games. Then, noting that the most noteworthy thing most retirees do is die, I re-entered the consulting business. Most of my sports travel these days consists of ten mile trips to Target Center, the Metrodome and Williams Arena, but I'll always make time for trips to the best games, stadiums and arenas, wherever they may be. As the book goes to press, my journey is in its fifty-first year, with 3180 games down and, hopefully, thousands more still to come.

GAME

Nassau Coliseum 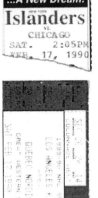**2232**

Chicago Blackhawks at New York Islanders

Los Angeles,   February 17, 1990

GAME

Great Western Forum **2233**

Quebec Nordiques at Los Angeles Kings

Time for Mary Beth and me to head to Southern California for the final February break of her high school years; the first half of our coast-to-coast doubleheader is in Long Island, using her Islanders season seats. Later that summer I told her: "I have two invoices here, one from the Islanders for your season ticket renewal, the other from Western New England College for your tuition; remarkably, they're not that different in amount; I'm not paying both." She made the right choice; now she has a college degree, a good job and her own apartment. She's no longer dependent on Dad, except for hockey tickets.

Philadelphia,   August 15, 1990

GAME

Veterans Stadium **2322**

San Francisco Giants at Philadelphia Phillies

Finally, a no hitter! After 45 seasons of baseball games I get to my first and only no hit game. In a season where no hitters were becoming commonplace, with two even accomplished the same night, I'm becoming increasingly embarrassed to admit I've never been present for a no hitter. Terry Mulholland's masterpiece against the Giants was a complete surprise, down to the final out. Very few strikeouts; the Giants were hitting the ball hard, but right at Phillies fielders. It seemed only a matter of time before the Giants would explode for a big inning. Even the final out of the game followed the same pattern. Gary Carter's line drive was backhanded out of the air by a diving Charlie Hayes at third base and the improbable had happened. Now I'm a complete baseball fan; I've seen a no hitter.

New Orleans,   September 10, 1990

GAME

2333 Louisiana Superdome

San Francisco 49ers at New Orleans Saints

Monday Night Football and the city of New Orleans is a combination that is as guaranteed a good time as sports offers. Throw in a last second 49er victory, and there's no doubt I got my money's worth on this trip; twice I've been to Saints games at the Superdome; both times the Saints had the lead and lost in the final minutes; both times I was rooting (albeit in my own quiet, inconspicuous way) for the visitors. Yet the Saints fans were as gracious in defeat (and not just because they have so much practice) as any I've ever seen. It's no secret that New Orleans is a great party city; what is less known is that their sports fans are among the most gracious, classiest fans I've found anywhere in my travels.

Philadelphia,   October 15, 1990

GAME

2353 Veterans Stadium

Minnesota Vikings at Philadelphia Eagles

Moving to the other end of the fan decorum scale, Veterans Stadium was the site of this Vikings-Eagles Monday night matchup. The 9pm kickoff on the East Coast for Monday Night Football helps to maximize the blood alcohol count in every stadium, especially the Vet. Most stadiums are careful to forbid fans entering the stadium from carrying liquor bottles and other contraband; security is never perfect, but at the Vet security must have taken this night off; two inebriated lowlives spent the game swigging from a quart bottle of bourbon; frustrated at an Eagle misplay in the third quarter, the bottle was hurled to the ground, smashing and spreading broken glass and bourbon everywhere. No problem; one of our neighbors reached into a tote bag beneath the seat and came out with a second, completely unopened quart bottle of bourbon for second half consumption. Many fine, well behaved people are Eagles fans; but this team does have more than its share of work to do at improving the atmosphere at home games; a drunken crowd lobbing snowballs at Santa Claus is perhaps amusing, but other antics of the riff raff at Eagles games are completely uncalled for.

EAST STANDS **3** GATE **G** SEC.
18 AISLE **25** ROW **09** SEAT

GAME

Tampa Stadium 2413

Buffalo Bills vs. New York Giants

SUNDAY, JANUARY 27, 1991
6:00 PM
GATES OPEN 3:00 PM
$150 ALL TAXES INCLUDED

NFL

SUPER BOWL XXV

T he next two Super Bowls are in my two home cities; the Jet Pack hard core arrives several days ahead and stays at a gulf front motel near my condo; they spend most of their time in Tampa, at such disreputable spots as the Yucatan Liquor Stand, a decadent, down-scale saloon/sports bar in which, reputedly, more than one of "America's Most Wanted" had been apprehended. Once again I lead the caravan on game day; since I've had Bucs tickets for years, I know the back ways to the stadium and where to set up a tailgate in a Sears lot across from the Stadium. The Gulf War was on, so security was exceptionally tight; even cameras and radios were forbidden at the game; guards with metal detectors frisked all entering spectators. How surprised and jealous I was when the Jet Packer next to me pulled out a portable radio; how did he get it into the Stadium? The radio went under his hat and he chose the shortest security guard, whose wand did not reach the top of his head. Because of the war, official word was that no air traffic would be allowed anywhere near the Stadium during the game. The crowd was therefore shocked, and momentarily frightened, when, during the Anthem, jets from McDill Air Force base roared over the stadium. Once settled in, they saw a classic football game, with the most dramatic finish I've ever witnessed; the Bills missed last second field goal would be as close as Buffalo would come in their four Super Bowls. The Jet Pack, all native New Yorkers, reveled in the Giants Super Bowl victory. All, that is, except Richie, the die hard AFC guy.

Sacramento, February 14, 1991

GAME
2419 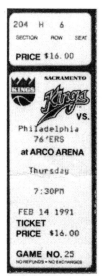 Arco Arena
Philadelphia 76ers at Sacramento Kings

I n the middle of nowhere, close to the Sacramento airport and nothing else, the Arco Arena is surprisingly full for the 76ers-Kings matchup. The Kings get out to a 15-0 lead; has there ever been a shutout in the NBA? Of course not, but thinking back to the days before the twenty-four second clock for low scoring games causes me to realize what I'm watching. Trace the history of these two wandering franchises and you end up on the New York Thruway, the Syracuse Nats and the Rochester Royals of my childhood; imagine these players to be Schayes, Arizin, Rocha, and Kerr, and the courtside fans to be farmers jamming pitchforks into opposing players venturing too close to the sideline. It helped my enjoyment of an otherwise uneventful game. In this fiftieth anniversary year of NBA basketball, its great to be old; I don't have to study the league's history, I remember it.

Edmonton, March 13, 1991

GAME
2438  Edmonton Coliseum
New York Islanders at Edmonton Oilers

M ary Beth is in college, so her annual hockey trip with Dad coincides with spring break. While classmates head for Daytona, Fort Lauderdale or other beaches, my daughter and I took a whirlwind five day NHL tour through Chicago, Minneapolis, Edmonton and Los Angeles. Her highlight is in, of all places, Edmonton; having given up her Islander season tickets, it is one of her rare opportunities to catch up with her favorite team.

**DIVISIONAL
PLAYOFF**

**DATE AND TIME
TO BE ANNOUNCED**

SEC   ROW   SEAT
201   13   6

5-39904

GAME

Metropolitan Sports Center **2460**

Chicago Blackhawks at Minnesota North Stars

I have season tickets to both of these teams, and miss very few home games of either; of the two, I think the Hawks have superior talent, and a much better shot at the Stanley Cup; but in this opening round, something strange happens; the Stars steal the opening game in overtime at Chicago; the Hawks seem increasingly unable to cope with the Stars tenacious style as the series continues; the Stars take the series in six games; the North Stars bandwagon has been loaded, and the Met Center is uncommonly full; I knew that both my teams couldn't continue in the playoffs since they faced each other in the opening round, but to my surprise it would be North Stars I'd be following all the way through to the finals this year.

St. Louis, April 20, 1991

GAMES

Busch Stadium **2464, 2466**

Philadelphia Phillies   (doubleheader)
at St. Louis Cardinals

GAME

St. Louis Arena **2465**

Minnesota North Stars at St. Louis Blues

Thanks to bad weather in the first week of the baseball season, the Cardinals had a twi-night doubleheader against the Phillies. I found a unique between games activity; leaving in the seventh inning of the first game, I took a cab to the Arena for the North Stars-Blues Stanley Cup playoff game; returning to the ball park after the game, the Phils and Cardinals were in the sixth inning of game two; they played ten innings with the Phillies winning to gain a split in the doubleheader; the only way this day would have been better would be if there had been a long between games ceremony and I could have missed fewer innings while at the hockey game.

Boston, May 9, 1991

GAME

2479 Boston Garden

Detroit Pistons at Boston Celtics

GAME

2480 Fenway Park

Texas Rangers at Boston Red Sox

GAME

2481 Boston Garden

Pittsburgh Penguins at Boston Bruins

The scheduling was too good to be true; the Celtics and Bruins shared the Garden, so with both in the playoffs, the Celtics had to play the Detroit Pistons at 1pm; the 8am flight from Minnesota got me to Causeway Street by noon, in plenty of time to see a thrilling 109-103 Celtics victory; after the game, I picked up a ticket for that night's Bruins game since I knew I would be a late arrival; knowing I'd not be around for the finish, I was in Fenway in time for batting practice; I have the Bruins on my radio while watching the Red Sox; it's the second inning and the anthem is being played at the Garden; where are these extra-long versions of the anthem the one time I need one? The Bruins and Penguins face off; the Red Sox and Texas finish four innings; the hockey game is midway in the first period. I'm on my way; it's only a five minute cab ride to the Garden; I catch the last five minutes of the first period and the remainder of the Bruins-Penguins game; I should have stayed at Fenway; the Bruins got pushed around in their own building in a very un-Bruinlike manner; the Penguins won 7-2 and the game wasn't even really that close; discussing this game a few weeks later with former Bruin coach Don Cherry, I mentioned how his Bruins might have been beaten but never pushed around in their own building. I had pushed the right button; I kept quiet and enjoyed Bruin stories from the great former coach turned TV star for a good hour.

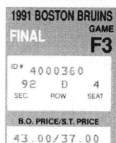

Philadelphia, May 10, 1991

GAME

Spectrum **2482**

Chicago Bulls at Philadelphia 76ers

It was probably the last great Sixers moment before the steady downslide of a once proud franchise that continues to this day. But in 1991 the Sixers still had enough talent and pride to put up a strong effort in a playoff series against the Chicago Bulls. Hersey Hawkins sent the fans home with a twenty foot buzzer-beater that gave the Sixers a 99-97 victory; Chicago won the series, but on this night for one last time the Sixers brought back memories of Chamberlain, Erving and the franchise's greats of the sixties and seventies.

Pittsburgh, May 23, 1991

GAME

Civic Arena 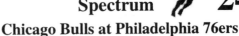 **2489**

Minnesota North Stars at Pittsburgh Penguins

Except for one of the games in Edmonton, I'd been to every North Stars playoff game, home and away; tonight would likely decide the Stanley Cup champion; the final series is tied two games apiece; the Penguins have overcome the mediocrity of their first twenty years in the NHL to emerge as an NHL powerhouse, led by the incomparable Mario Lemieux; they were probably the most talented team in the league, but couldn't shake these irritating, close checking, opportunistic North Stars; game six would be in Minnesota two nights hence and tonight's winning team would have a chance to capture the Cup; naturally I was hoping that the North Stars would be winners, but had brought two extra tickets to game six to Pittsburgh with me, knowing that, should Pittsburgh win, these tickets would have much greater value to Penguin fans than to the Minnesotans; the North Stars played well, but in the end, the better team won; delirious fans swarmed out of the arena celebrating the 6-4 Penguin victory; one fan near me was shouting to his family: We're going, we're going, I'll get them, I don't know how but I'll get them. Could he be referring to game six tickets, I inquired? Yes, do you have any. Yes, I replied, right here; I don't have any cash on me said my new friend but I can go to a cash machine and meet you in an hour. Fine, I said, see you at the bar at the William Penn Hotel. An hour later he was back and with no negotiation, put more cash on the bar than two North Star tickets had ever commanded. Unknown to the buyer, 650 miles to the west the market was crashing, as the Minnesota "faithful", sensing a Penguins Stanley Cup, were evacuating the North Stars bandwagon as though it were the Titanic.

Minneapolis, May 25, 1991

GAME

2491  Metropolitan Sports Center

Pittsburgh Penguins at Minnesota North Stars

STANLEY CUP CHAMPIONSHIP

DATE AND TIME TO BE ANNOUNCED

SEC	ROW	SEAT
201	13	6

5-39904

H ad the Stars, not the Penguins, been up three games to two and about to capture the Stanley Cup, Minnesotans by the thousands would have been petitioning the Governor demanding that more tickets be made available for "long-suffering, loyal" fans (who of course spent most of the Stars twenty five year history disguised as empty seats). But the Penguins victory in game six turned the Stars' fans back to their accustomed indifferent mode. All the seats were sold at the Met, but many were not occupied. Worse yet, as it became apparent the Penguins would win the Cup as they cruised to an 8-0 rout of the North Stars, fans by the thousands left the arena. I have to believe they knew that the traditional Stanley Cup ceremony would take place in the building shortly; for all the years I've followed the NHL I've seen that ceremony only four times; any fan with any respect for the game of hockey would stay for the ceremony, whether their favorite team was winning the Cup or not. And, furthermore, the North Stars had over-achieved in this 1990-91 season, and deserved a far better salute from the home fans than the sounds of pick-up truck ignitions starting the race out of the parking lot. Stars' coaching was brilliant, the offense opportunistic, goaltending and penalty killing outstanding; but their fan demographics needed work, lots of work; I doubt any of the departing "North Star faithful" had ever seen the Stanley Cup presented; the next season the Stars' dramatic Stanley Cup run was acknowledged with the sale of a pathetic six thousand season tickets (despite the fact that the team's prices were the lowest in the league). The handwriting was on the wall for my adopted home team; it would not be long before all my NHL games would be road games.

GAME

Wrigley Field  **2495**
Pittsburgh Pirates at Chicago Cubs

Fourth of July at Wrigley, and a beautiful day for a ball game; hordes of people fill the neighborhood streets; tickets are at a premium; a young girl asks me if I need tickets, because her Dad has some; she leads me to her Dad, an entrepreneurial urban street person with more game tickets than teeth; Dad tells the daughter "Why did you bring this guy to me. Don't you know he buys only good seats? All I have left are in the upper deck;" I left to find another scalper, impressed at this hustler's ability to memorize and categorize customers and prospects, and pleased that I was known as a discriminating consumer of Chicago sports events.

Chicago, September 23, 1991

GAME

Soldier Field  **2504**
New York Jets at Chicago Bears

The Jet Pack doesn't travel to all the away games, but a Monday night matchup in Chicago is irresistable; the pre game drill was only slightly more restrained than the annual pre-Super Bowl experience. I joined the group on Monday afternoon, after they spent the weekend at Notre Dame, Wrigley Field, Chicago Stadium and half the bars and saloons enroute. To commemorate Richie's devoted leadership and unflagging loyalty to the Jets, I prepared a proclamation, to be presented at half-time; the joke was that the award was formatted as a subpoena, on an official looking form obtainable at any stationery store; a dozen of us sat together in good seats in a corner of Soldier Field; we enlisted the help of a Bears fan seated some distance from Richie, and asked him to come by at halftime and "serve" the subpoena on our beloved leader of the Pack. Most Jet Packers know a subpoena when they see one, but a reasonable facsimile produces a few seconds of irrational fear; the joke worked even better than we could imagine; in the third quarter, a Bears fan seated behind Richie, his face pale with fear, tapped Richie on the shoulder and asked: "Did you get served, here?" We could read his mind; his adversary be it a creditor, ex-wife or the long arm of the law could trace him through his season tickets. I don't doubt that he voluntarily asked the Bears for a fifteen yard penalty in his seat location in the interest of lying low. As usual, the Jets disappointed the Pack; a potential game winning field goal was missed; the Bears won by a field goal just seconds before the fifteen minute overtime would have expired. It was past 1am alongside Lake Michigan when the tailgate was adjourned; a few of the Pack were hitting the road immediately for a sixteen hour drive back to Long Island; the hard core headed for Division Street, where last call comes around 4am.

Minneapolis, October 26, 1991

GAME

2519 Metropolitan Sports Center

Boston Bruins at Minnesota North Stars

GAME

2520 Metrodome

Atlanta Braves at Minnesota Twins

The North Stars played in the afternoon, because game six of the World Series was in Minneapolis that evening; the Atlanta Braves were on the verge of winning the World Series; standing in their way, the upstart Minnesota Twins, a gutsy, overachieving group who ignore local whining that the big markets get the best players; they just go out and play the game; play the game in a ridiculous, carpeted dome perfect for football, but play it well nonetheless. The Twins would accomplish in their "disadvantaged small market" their second World Championship in five seasons, more than the large market Cubs and White Sox have posted in their last 150! It's not how much revenue you have, it's how you use it; this was Kirby Puckett's finest night, a game saving catch in the top of the eleventh followed by a game winning home run in the bottom half; 11 innings, the World Series tied at three games apiece, one of the classic games ever and the best in my fifty years at the game.

San Francisco, November 12, 1991

GAME

2526 Cow Palace

Buffalo Sabres at San Jose Sharks

I enter the parking lot reflecting in amazement how this arena that over thirty-five years ago I thought woefully inadequate and minor league has not only survived but is now the (temporary) home of a National Hockey League franchise. Oddly, what once seemed obsolete now was refreshingly different and charming, unlike the newer generation of arenas and stadiums, each one a replica of the next. In the hallway, I lingered over the pictures of the great events in the history of the Cow Palace; political conventions, rodeos, basketball, roller derby and of course, as the name suggests, livestock shows were all chronicled along the corridors of the odd looking building. My two Sharks games this week were a welcome step back in time, not because of hockey, because of this unique arena.

Metrodome  **2556**

Buffalo Bills vs. Washington Redskins

The Jet Pack comes to Minnesota! The metro area is large enough that I found them a hotel quite INconvenient to my home; two North Stars games, a Timberwolves game and all the NFL festivities occupied the three days leading up to the game; the 1am curfew at downtown pubs was met with disbelief by chagrinned Jet Packers who, for the most part were on their first trip to Minnesota. The game itself was a good matchup; not all of the Jet Pack seats are together, so the matching of people and locations was an important task, accomplished in executive session of the most senior (and sober) Jet Packers at my home the night before the game; I was assigned to sit with a security chief from one of the NFL teams (probably because my behavior was deemed least likely to attract his attention, professionally speaking). The Redskin team, and hundreds of its fans, occupied a suburban hotel close to my home; across the hotel parking lot is a popular outlet of a well-known national restaurant chain; predictably, hundreds of delirious revelers, chanting "Hail to the Redskins" for the thousandth time descended on the restaurant about 10pm for post game food and drinks; fortunately, my party got through the doors just ahead of the onslaught; two hours and six rounds of drinks later our food still had not been served; the restaurant was bedlam; an apologetic manager explained that since business was so slow about 8pm he sent most of the staff home early, completely forgetting that the Super Bowl on the bar TV was being played ten miles away, and that the winning team and its fans were all staying in the adjacent hotel. He explained that shortly after we arrived they started turning would-be diners away. Even Mark Rypien, the Redskins quarterback, who an hour earlier was voted MVP of the Super Bowl, was denied service at this restaurant; how fleeting can fame be? Even before leaving for Disney World, Mark Rypien's stature is diminished by a Minnesota maitre'd oblivious to football; a year later he is Vinnie Testaverde's back-up; his career is in a free fall.

Honolulu, February 2, 1992

GAME

2557 Aloha Stadium

I certainly deserve to be chosen for Pro Bowl as a fan; in the preceding six seasons I've attended 145 NFL games, including five Super Bowls; actually this is my fourth consecutive Pro Bowl, but the first at which part of the Jet Pack was involved; the Jet Pack normally heads for warm climates following Super Bowl, usually Mexico or the Caribbean; the over/under on their return to New York hovers somewhere around the third of March. But this year I've convinced the Leader of the Pack to head for Hawaii. Like many geographically ignorant New Yorkers he figures Minnesota is about 80% of the way to Hawaii anyway (the actual progress is 20%) so why not take in Pro Bowl this year; Pro Bowl is the most low key football game anywhere; players appreciate their Hawaiian vacation and the honor of their selection; the last thing they want to do is hurt one another; fans sport the colors of all NFL teams in roughly equal proportions and the game result or point differential is of interest to only the most pathological of handicappers. My mistake was allowing Richie to get the tickets; remember, he's a yard-line guy. We definitely were on the fifty, or more correctly, in orbit somewhere above the fifty; one of our group is quite nearsighted; I gave him my zoom binoculars, but they were little help; he couldn't have seen the players with an observatory telescope. Fortunately not much worth seeing happens on the Pro Bowl field. Did the AFC win? Who can remember? Probably only Richie; not only is he a yard line guy, he's an AFC guy to the end.

The Jet Pack assembles in Miami for another Super Bowl

GAME 31

$27.00

VS
DETROIT
Sun., Feb. 23, 1992
1:35 p.m.

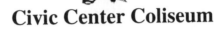

Hartford, February 23, 1992
GAME
Civic Center Coliseum 2565
Detroit Red Wings at Hartford Whalers

Long Island, February 23, 1992
GAME
Nassau Coliseum 2566
Washington Capitals at New York Islanders

New York, February 23, 1992
GAME
Madison Square Garden 2567
Philadelphia Flyers at New York Rangers

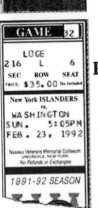

GAME 32

LOGE
2 16   L   6
SEC   ROW   SEAT
PRICE $35.00 Tax Included

New York ISLANDERS
vs.
WASHINGTON
SUN.   5:05PM
FEB. 23, 1992

Nassau Veterans Memorial Coliseum
UNIONDALE, NEW YORK
No Refunds or Exchanges

1991-92 SEASON

TOWER GATE SECTION
B   72   313
ROW   SEAT   GAME
F   9   #30
$22.00   INCLUDING TAX

NEW YORK
RANGERS

S ome years ago, a quirk in the NHL schedule had the three New York area teams at home the same night; a few fans managed to attend one period each of the Devils, Rangers and Islanders the same night; I regarded that as sort of a senseless stunt, inasmuch as the fans didn't see very much of any game. But it gave me the idea of trying to see three COMPLETE NHL games in a single day, and each year I would scrutinize the schedule to find such an opportunity. Finally, it became possible; leaving my Long Island hotel about 10am, I was in downtown Hartford in plenty of time for a 130pm faceoff; I did have to sacrifice the third period of the Whalers game in the interest of getting to the two other games; at the start of the second intermission, I sped out of the Hartford garage, heading for Long Island and a 505pm face off at the Coliseum; I walked in as the National Anthem was being played; following the game I drove to the nearby train station at Mineola and got a train due to arrive in Penn Station, directly below the Garden, at 840pm; I expected to miss the faceoff, but as so often happens when multiple events are at the Garden, the ice was not ready; I was in my seat at the Garden when the puck dropped at 845pm; the Flyers and Rangers even played extra time, the Rangers getting the game winner in overtime. A full day of hockey, my unique "hat trick".

Toronto, February 29,1992

GAME

2572  Maple Leaf Gardens

Chicago Blackhawks at Toronto Maple Leafs

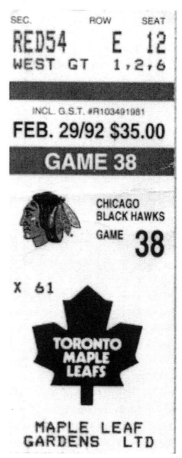

RED54   E 12
WEST GT 1,2,6

INCL. G.S.T. #R103491981

FEB. 29/92 $35.00

GAME 38

CHICAGO
BLACK HAWKS
GAME 38

X 61

TORONTO
MAPLE
LEAFS

MAPLE LEAF
GARDENS LTD

Anyone who believes hockey can ever achieve acceptability in the United States comparable to the Canadian appreciation of the game is beyond naive, and has certainly never spent a Saturday in Toronto during hockey season. Every Canadian grows up with the local hockey rink as a focal point of community activity; and if the neighborhood rink is the parish church, Maple Leaf Gardens is the Vatican. Even in hockey-aware regions of Michigan, Minnesota and Massachusetts, the rink is just another place where some people play their game; hockey shares attention with baseball, basketball and football; everyone is familiar with those games; a minority of zealots, myself among them, grow up with a love of hockey; but it can not compare with the linkage between the hockey rink and what it means to be Canadian. Chicago is a great hockey market, one of the best, but there is more widespread awareness of the visiting Blackhawks, their history, their players, their coach, their goaltending, their injuries, and their strategy here in Toronto than in Chicago; the same goes for any team coming in to meet the Leafs on a Saturday night before a huge national television audience; no detail goes unnoticed; in Chicago (and in Boston, New York and other good American hockey cities), the game itself goes unnoticed by the majority of the population. Regardless of the fortunes of the Leafs, Toronto is the most hockey-savvy city in the world; with the demise of the other legendary buildings, Maple Leaf Gardens is now my most frequent stop on the NHL tour.

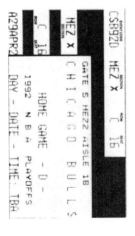

GAME

Comiskey Park **2605**

Boston Red Sox at Chicago White Sox

GAME

Chicago Stadium  **2606**

New York Knicks at Chicago Bulls

I enjoy an afternoon at the new Comiskey watching two glorious old franchises, the Sox, in a rivalry that predates my birth by forty years. But the big event in Chicago this night is the Bulls-Knicks playoff game. I buy a ticket from a man whose excitement level is near Jet Pack proportions. He is so up for the game he can barely talk. Knowing that Bulls fans are the most opportunistic in sports, nowhere to be found for decades but rabid in their dedication providing the team is the best in the world, I inquire: "You're quite a fan; how long have you been following the Bulls?" "Five long years, man, five years". Figures. Before Michael Jordan arrived, Bulls fans were almost as scarce as Angels fans. "How about you, are you a Bulls fan", he asks. I tell him I'm really neutral, but that I still remember in 1953 when Harry Gallatin, Carl Braun, Ernie Vandeweghe, Vince Boryla and others of the early Knicks put on a clinic at my school; even forty years later, that memory has more impact on me than anything the Bulls have done; diplomatically, I told him I expected the Bulls to win the series (which of course they did), but even though the Knicks persona has, shall we say, changed dramatically, I still carry a lingering attachment to the orange and blue.

Chicago, June 1, 1992

GAME

2613  Chicago Stadium

Pittsburgh Penguins at Chicago Blackhawks

The Hawks 1991 team was probably a more legitimate Stanley Cup threat but for their ambush by the over-achieving, underappreciated Minnesota North Stars; but this year's team was good enough to get to the finals and get a three goal lead in game one at Pittsburgh; then it all came apart for the Hawks, blowing the lead in game one and going down to defeat in four straight; it has been thirty-one years since the last Hawk Cup championship, and most of the loyalists at the Stadium either remember the 1961 team or have heard about it from their parents; one particularly boisterous man seated near me, with the official Indian head crest on his jersey kept insisting to me that he had been at the Stadium when the Hawks won the 1961 Cup; I pointed out that he must have felt lonely, since the deciding game was played in Detroit; but he swore he saw the Cup in Chicago Stadium; the last time the Hawks won the Cup at home was 1938, before either of us was born; finally, we realized that he must have been at the 1971 final, when Montreal won the Cup in Chicago. Once again a visiting team captain, this time Mario Lemieux, skated around the Stadium ice with the Cup; the still packed Chicago Stadium saluted the Penguins with a deafening level of cheering normally reserved for the National Anthem and Hawk victories. Quite a contrast from last year.

Cleveland, September 14, 1992

GAME

2622 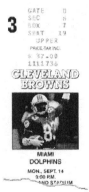 Cleveland Stadium

Miami Dolphins at Cleveland Browns

Monday Night Football at Cleveland Stadium; it gets no better than this; the front of the upper deck in the old stadium on the lakefront had the best views in the NFL, both of the game and the downtown skyline a few blocks away; I saw the Browns play surprisingly well on a number of Monday nights, upsetting the Bears and 49ers on two of my previous Mondays in Cleveland; this night, they give the Dolphins a good battle, but Miami gets a 27-23 victory. I had no idea this would be my last time at the great old stadium; the thought of the Browns not being in Cleveland was, if anything, even more absurd than imagining the Colts out of Baltimore and the Dodgers out of Brooklyn; but the Browns were allowed to escape to Baltimore; the NFL will one day return to Cleveland, and their team will even carry the Browns name; but the people of Cleveland will suffer needless loss, and the community will pay even more to get a team back than it would have taken to keep them from leaving in the first place. First Brooklyn, then Baltimore, then Cleveland; it is a lesson that shouldn't have to be learned the hard way, but I'm afraid that Cleveland will not be the last place to suffer this kind of loss; that's a good reason for fans not to become too attached to any one team.

GAME

Expo Hall 2642

Winnipeg Jets at Tampa Bay Lightning

The NHL has come to Florida and for this one season the expansion Lightning are playing in a converted pig barn on the State Fair Grounds; in its one season, more comical things happened in this one building than in the lifetime of many others; whenever a Canadian team visited, one would think fans had to clear customs to go to their seats, so many Canadian flags were in evidence; but the Canadians didn't buy season tickets; native Floridians filled the sidelines, paying premium prices for seats "on the fifty yard line"; of course, this isn't a football stadium, it is a pig barn; and from the sideline seats, views are extremely limited to the left and right; apparently, the natives never caught on; at the end of the rink was a ten row section with perfect sight lines; my season tickets were there; no native Floridians could be found; the transplants who knew hockey congregated where the game could be seen and patiently explained why, for example, octopi were flying on the ice during Detroit visits; security was so humorless it was as funny as the Keystone Cops; sheriff's deputies in "smoky" hats, carrying billy clubs patrolled the arena; an opening night hat trick caused the ejection of the first hat thrower; only the intervention of a hockey-knowledgeable team official saved the fan from execution by firing squad; take the wrong route to your seat and your path would be blocked by an intimidating officer; only one problem with security: at the back of the building, near a pond and the visitors locker room was an entry that was completely unguarded all season; since I parked behind the building, I always entered by the back door; I would have to seek out someone to tear my ticket; many others knew about the back door, very few of them ticket holders. A number of Floridians nearly froze to death on their first visit; with eighty degree outdoor temperatures common, people dressed accordingly; but to keep the ice playable, the temperature inside the arena was lower than in, say, Montreal. More than once I saw highly distressed fans (presumably at their first game) asking for blanket rentals at the concession stands.

Pasadena, January 31, 1993

GAME

2678 Rose Bowl

Buffalo Bills vs.
Dallas Cowboys

C 07 15 009
GATE TUNNEL ROW SEAT

AFC-NFC WORLD CHAMPIONSHIP GAME
SUNDAY, JANUARY 31, 1993 • 3:00 PM
ROSE BOWL • PASADENA, CALIFORNIA

NFL $175 ALL TAXES INCLUDED
GATES OPEN AT 12:00 PM

SUPER BOWL XXVII

O nce again, it's Super Bowl with the Jet Pack; headquartered by the beach in Manhattan Beach, there's plenty of night life to be found; Richie wins an Elvis lookalike contest without even knowing he has been entered; the prize is a free night of drinking for his party the following night; very dangerous for the financial solvency of the bar. I break away from the group from time to time to take in a Kings game and other Southern California attractions, causing my blood alcohol count to drop below required Jet Pack minimums. By game time, many of the Jet Packers are near exhaustion; yet this annual near-death experience leads up to a game involving teams the Jet Pack doesn't really care about. What would happen to these party animals if the Jets were actually playing in a Super Bowl; some just couldn't handle it, and would probably implode from excitement and crumble to earth like a building being demolished. Fortunately, the Jets show no signs of Super Bowl participation within the actuarial life expectancy of these aged teenagers.

Q *UESTION FREQUENTLY ASKED OF THE AUTHOR:*
Why don't you work in sports?

Only two jobs in sports pay well, player and owner. My resume qualifies me to be neither; almost without exception, all other sports employees are underpaid, overworked and have no control over their schedules. I want the freedom to follow basketball today, baseball tomorrow, to change my mind enroute to the Toronto Maple Leafs and watch the Maryland Terrapins instead. No job in sports would let me do that!

Sarasota, March 16, 1993

GAME

Ed Smith Stadium  2696

Florida Marlins at Chicago White Sox

Tampa, March 16, 1993

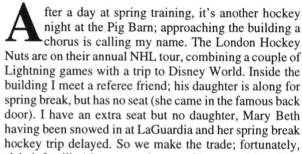

GAME

Expo Hall **2697**

Hartford Whalers at
Tampa Bay Lightning

After a day at spring training, it's another hockey night at the Pig Barn; approaching the building a chorus is calling my name. The London Hockey Nuts are on their annual NHL tour, combining a couple of Lightning games with a trip to Disney World. Inside the building I meet a referee friend; his daughter is along for spring break, but has no seat (she came in the famous back door). I have an extra seat but no daughter, Mary Beth having been snowed in at LaGuardia and her spring break hockey trip delayed. So we make the trade; fortunately, most hockey officials (and their families) have a good sense of humor; with no idea who this girl was, the nearby fans were unrestrained in their second guessing of the officiating; Jack the Ripper, O.J.Simpson and Adolf Hitler, combined, could not generate the animosity that one NHL referee can produce in a crowd far more emotional than analytical; it would be interesting to know if the remarks would have been different had the identity of the young lady seated nearby had been known by the raging rednecks.

QUESTION FREQUENTLY ASKED OF THE AUTHOR:

Besides the major team sports, what others do you follow?

I enjoy tennis, and have been to the U.S. Open and other tournaments; I have some interest in boxing, particularly the sport's rich history; otherwise I ignore (and am ignorant of) horse racing, wrestling, auto racing, bungee jumping, archery, dwarf throwing, volleyball and the dozens of other team and individual sports. Because I'm ignorant of these sports, I make no editorial comment or suggestions about them. Too bad the meddling know-nothings can not extend the same courtesy to my favorite sport, NHL hockey.

Minneapolis, April 13, 1993

GAME

2721 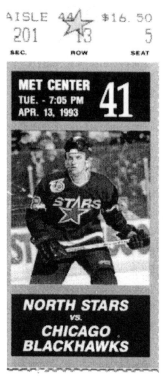 Metropolitan Sports Center

Chicago Blackhawks at Minnesota North Stars

AISLE 44 $16.50
201 13 5
SEC. ROW SEAT

MET CENTER
TUE. - 7:05 PM
APR. 13, 1993
41

NORTH STARS
VS.
CHICAGO
BLACKHAWKS

It's a sad night in Minnesota. The North Stars will move to Dallas next season; within a year, this perfect hockey building will be dynamited into history. On this night, chants of "Norm Green Sucks", the new Minnesota state motto, fill the air; locals put the blame on the team's owner; Green was less than a model citizen but the failure of NHL hockey in Minnesota isn't explained that simply. There's plenty of blame to be shared; the Minnesota business community never purchased blocks of season tickets and suites, even though many Minnesota-based corporations owned season tickets and luxury suites at other NHL arenas; tickets were priced were so low that even sellout crowds produced minimal revenue. The nucleus of devoted fans who bought season tickets with their own money and supported the team for decades are, as usual, the innocent victims; some argue that the competition from college and high school hockey hurt the Stars; yet in Massachusetts and Michigan hockey flourishes at all three levels; and anyone who can't distinguish between high school and the NHL is, hopefully, not spending money on any hockey tickets; furthermore, even in Minnesota, football and basketball are supported at all three levels. Why not hockey? It is a perplexing question; when the Winnipeg Jets wanted to relocate to Minneapolis, the cool civic reception sent the team to Phoenix instead; one could hardly blame the NHL for giving up on returning to Minnesota, yet there may still be hope; regrettably, it may be a team much like the Stars, abandoning its own loyal fans to look for a better deal. Will the NHL ever return in Minnesota? I hope so, but it would be the second biggest trick in the book; the biggest being filling the arena once the team arrives; remember the wisdom of Yogi: "If the fans are determined to stay home, there's no way you're going to stop them!"

GAME

Dodger Stadium  **2736**

Colorado Rockies at L.A. Dodgers

GAME

Great **2737**
Western Forum
Toronto Maple Leafs
at Los Angeles Kings

I'm often asked about the cost of game tickets; my concern is more with the cost of plane tickets, because even the priciest event normally costs less than the air fare; an exception to this rule occurred when Northwest offered a hundred dollar promotion between Minneapolis and Los Angeles at the same time the Kings made a run at the Stanley Cup and after a quarter century of anonymity became the hottest ticket in town. The Leafs and Kings were both over-achieving; one would get to the Stanley Cup finals; it was a hard fought entertaining series, this Sunday night clash at the Forum no exception. My game ticket cost me slightly more than my total travel cost; of course, among the many advantages of traveling out of Minneapolis are the "red-eye" flights home from all the West Coast cities, departing a couple of hours after games end. So my travel costs for the day were airfare, car rental, and parking; no hotel needed, just a delightful day trip to LA.

Los Angeles,   June 5, 1993
GAME

2738 Great Western Forum

Montreal Canadiens at Los Angeles Kings

It was the Los Angeles Kings twenty-sixth season in the National Hockey League; yet the morning of game three of the 1993 Stanley Cup finals, a local newspaper printed an extra insert with an introduction to hockey for those unfamiliar with the game. That newspaper insert speaks volumes about the indifference with which Southern California treated their NHL team for a quarter century and the sudden hysteria about hockey as the Kings seemed on their way to becoming Stanley Cup champions; the series was tied at a game apiece as the Stanley Cup Finals moved to California; interest in this game was as high as I've seen for any event, including Super Bowls; reportedly, four former Presidents of the United States attended the game: Reagan, Bush, Ford and Nixon. I'm not sure whether that report was true; Ronald Reagan's entourage was seated at ice level, directly across from my seat; the gentlemen behind him wearing headsets were definitely not assistant coaches communicating with scouts in the press box; I did not see any of the other three former Commanders in Chief, but the event was of such stature that the report was believable, accurate or not. During the Stanley Cup finals, the Cup is displayed in the participating cities and, of course, when a team achieves four victories, awarded to the winning team. During the actual game this day, the Cup was locked in the game officials' dressing room, an oversized closet along a corridor just beneath the seats on the gold side of the Forum. The key was held by the standby referee, who asked me if I'd like my picture taken holding the Cup; I would have opted to have a picture taken with Ronald Reagan if I had a choice, but there are limits even to a referee's jurisdiction; so I posed holding the Cup; with a new ring of names added each year, the Cup has become surprisingly heavy; this explains why the members of the winning team when skating around with the Cup never take more than one lap before handing the Cup to a teammate. The photo came out so well I used it as a holiday greeting card in 1993; the game did not turn out as well for the Kings crowd, as the Canadiens John Le Clair scored the overtime game winner; the Kings Cup hopes ended the following Wednesday; within two seasons, the Great Western Forum was once again occupied principally by empty seats.

GAME

Oriole Park at Camden Yards 2753

Seattle Mariners at Baltimore Orioles

Most of the stadiums built in the last thirty years do not impress me as much as the one they replaced. Not so at Camden Yards, a magnificent ball park surrounded by restaurants and tourist attractions in the midst of the revitalized Inner Harbor area of downtown Baltimore; on this, my first visit, I realized that even someone with no interest in baseball would enjoy a visit to Camden Yards, so much entertainment exists both inside and just outside the ballpark itself. I sat in a prime lower deck seat behind first base, and had a wonderful view; I did note that a large number, perhaps as many as twenty thousand, seats at Camden Yards are in the outfield; some of those are even sold as luxury suites, but if you sat there and caught a ball it would be a home run! The constant sellouts at Oriole Park confirm that many who don't mind watching from a great distance still consider it worthwhile to buy high-priced Oriole tickets, even in the outfield.

BASEBALL GAME SUMMARY: (through 5/19/97)

National League reg. season......311	**Most Frequent Home Teams**
American League reg. season....271	
Spring Training 96	New York Mets........129
National League post season 8	Minnesota Twins......106
World Series................................8	Philadelphia Phillies...55
American League post season 7	Boston Red Sox..........52
Minor Leagues 4	New York Yankees 52

TOTAL:.......................705

Chicago,   October 6, 1993

GAME

2766 Comiskey Park

Toronto Blue Jays at Chicago White Sox

GAME

2767 Chicago Stadium

Florida Panthers at Chicago Blackhawks

O pening night at the final season for my favorite indoor arena, Chicago Stadium. My air and hotel bookings were set for the Hawks season before the White Sox won the Western Division and advanced to the American League Championship Series; so I got a bonus, post-season baseball all afternoon; Comiskey Park was officially "sold out", but an interesting economics lesson was unfolding on 35th Street before the game. Many tickets were available on the street, in part I'm sure due to the game being played on a weekday afternoon; but in searching for a suitable ticket, I soon found that lower seats between the bases were as scarce as Kings tickets in the Stanley Cup Finals; on the other hand, upper level ticket holders were having as much trouble getting rid of their extras as the man in Atlanta who won a bet by giving away a ticket fifteen years earlier; the reason should be obvious on anyone's first visit to Comiskey; the lower level seats between the bases are excellent; but the lowest row of the upper level is about as high as the roof of old Comiskey Park since the luxury suites and press level sit between the lower and upper decks; people would pay a good premium for lower boxes, if they could be found; but upper level tickets were impossible to dispose of. This supply and demand marketplace confirmed vividly the discrepancy between the ten thousand or so good seats and the remainder of the stadium. The Blue Jays won the game, and ultimately the Series; that evening the expansion Florida Panthers played their first game, a 4-4 tie with the Hawks; their third year in the league the Panthers got to the Stanley Cup finals. No such good fortune in Chicago; perhaps it is because the Cubs, White Sox, Bears and Hawks have undying year-in, year-out fan support despite their lack of post-season success.

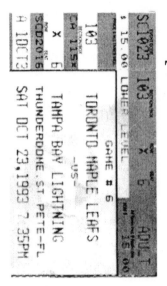

GAME

Thunderdome 🏒 **2775**

Toronto Maple Leafs
at Tampa Bay Lightning

I've endured baseball in a dome as long as I've lived in Minnesota; dome football can be appealing, especially late in the season in Minnesota; the Timberwolves played in a dome their first year in the NBA, so I'm not unfamiliar with domed stadiums. But hockey in a dome is absolutely too weird. The Lightning, after a year in the tiny pig barn have gone to the other extreme and moved into a fifty thousand seat baseball stadium; the only advantage of this "rink" is location; the Dome roof is visible from my condo, three miles to the West by the Gulf of Mexico; so getting to and from the game is easy, but getting a good view once inside is impossible. People sit in the second and third levels, seats which are at a long distance even for baseball; but the downstairs level has such a gradual slope that there is no elevation above the rink until about 25 rows from the baseball field; to make matters worse, the rink itself is not close to any seats, except temporary rinkside bleachers, some of which are good, if not luxurious, locations; officials walk out of the tunnel and along a mat leading to the pitchers mound; the rink extends from the pitchers mound out to the baseball outfield; fortunately, this was only a temporary home for the Lightning, and they have since moved into a very good hockey building, the Ice Palace in Tampa. The Lightning crowds in the Dome were, if this can be believed, even less knowledgeable than at the Fair Grounds the previous season; many upper level seats were sold for just a few dollars, to show good attendance figures and maximize the concession sales; the game was of little consequence to many of the fans; of course, since the Leafs were the visitors, early-arriving snowbirds made their allegiance well known. It was a great day for Canadian teams in domes; the Leafs beat the Lightning; while eating dinner later at a local sports bar, we watched Joe Carter's World Series winning home run at Sky Dome as the Blue Jays defeated the Phillies in the 1993 World Series.

San Jose, February 11, 1994

GAME

2806 San Jose Arena

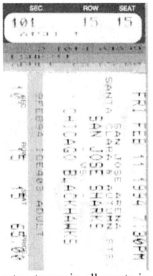

Chicago Blackhawks at
San Jose Sharks

I
t is as close to perfect as any of the new indoor arenas. The second deck starts at much lower elevation above the floor than in most new buildings; the lower level is surrounded by a private club, with the arena concourse accessed at the top of the lower level and the club from entryways thirteen rows above ice level. The Sharks have sold out over 100 consecutive games, and are one of the top teams in all sports in merchandise sales; fans not only buy tickets, a high percentage wear the official Sharks jersey to the game; fans are exuberant, but generally in an unoffensive way. They have a naive enthusiasm and attachment to their team way out of proportion to the Sharks' on-ice accomplishments. The Sharks fans personify the market the NHL is trying to reach: young, affluent, and for the most part, with limited understanding of the sport's history and traditions; even the most ardent Sharks fan would admit that Toronto and Boston hockey fans are, fan for fan, far more knowledgeable. Why then do the Sharks sell out every game with fans who cheer every move of a sub-par team, while on the same night in Toronto and Boston, thousands of tickets go unused, and the most frequently heard cheer is a loud chant of BORING, BORING! What will happen in the (unlikely) event that the Sharks fans become as discriminating as those in the "Original Six" cities? Will the NHL expand and expand, spreading talent even more thinly, making games even more boring, limiting the impact of diminished revenues by collecting huge expansion fees? What happens when all the logical and illogical expansion sites are taken? It won't be long. The NHL already has an expansion application from an area in whose airport an NHL official was once detained by a security guard who detected "shoes with razor blades attached" in the official's luggage. Hint: the city in question is not Hamilton, Ontario!

13 E 7
BOX ROW SEAT

USE RAMP No. 1

BOX $12.00

FT. LAUDERDALE STADIUM
Ft. Lauderdale, Florida

MARCH | WEDNESDAY

16 | MAR. 16
1994-1:05P.M.

RAIN CHECK
If 4½ innings are not completed, this check must be used for the re-scheduled game only. No exchange.
Knox-Staples-Brown, Inc., N.Y.

121 C 6
SEC. ROW SEAT
$55.00

VS.

CALGARY
FLAMES

MIAMI
ARENA
WED., MAR. 16, 1994
7:35 PM

GAME 32

Fort Lauderdale Stadium 2821

Detroit Tigers at New York Yankees

Miami, March 16, 1994

GAME

Miami Arena 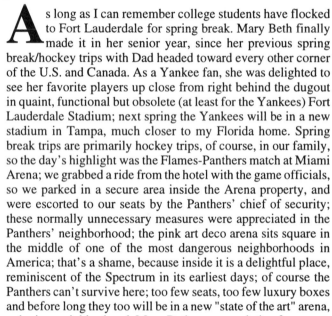 2822

Calgary Flames at Florida Panthers

As long as I can remember college students have flocked to Fort Lauderdale for spring break. Mary Beth finally made it in her senior year, since her previous spring break/hockey trips with Dad headed toward every other corner of the U.S. and Canada. As a Yankee fan, she was delighted to see her favorite players up close from right behind the dugout in quaint, functional but obsolete (at least for the Yankees) Fort Lauderdale Stadium; next spring the Yankees will be in a new stadium in Tampa, much closer to my Florida home. Spring break trips are primarily hockey trips, of course, in our family, so the day's highlight was the Flames-Panthers match at Miami Arena; we grabbed a ride from the hotel with the game officials, so we parked in a secure area inside the Arena property, and were escorted to our seats by the Panthers' chief of security; these normally unnecessary measures were appreciated in the Panthers' neighborhood; the pink art deco arena sits square in the middle of one of the most dangerous neighborhoods in America; that's a shame, because inside it is a delightful place, reminiscent of the Spectrum in its earliest days; of course the Panthers can't survive here; too few seats, too few luxury boxes and before long they too will be in a new "state of the art" arena, undoubtedly in a much nicer neighborhood. Mary Beth was completing four years in which her home hockey club was the Springfield Indians, so any NHL game was an exciting experience for her. She was less impressed by the team mascot, the Panther, who showed far more interest in her than vice versa. The Panther is just another in the long line of lame animal acts appearing at big league sports. Apart from two true comics, the Timberwolves' mascot Crunch and the Phillie Phanatic, I can't see any mascot making a difference in a team's ticket sales. Our evening concludes at former Flyer Rosie Paiement's sports bar named, appropriately, the Penalty Box. Where else would hockey officials to go for post-game entertainment?

Anaheim, April 11, 1994

GAME

2842 Anaheim Stadium
Cleveland Indians at California Angels

GAME

2843 Arrowhead Pond of Anaheim
Calgary Flames at Anaheim Mighty Ducks

I've carried all the sports schedules for many years, and always referred to them before confirming business appointments; of course, I've not had complete control over my schedule and would have to accept some assignments regardless of whether local teams were playing at home. Such was the case when I was asked to conduct a seminar at a very specific time and place, 4 to 6 p.m. Monday April 11; I accepted the assignment and only then checked the schedules; the seminar was at a hotel in Anaheim. The Angels opening day game was at 1pm; the Mighty Ducks had a home game at 8pm. I couldn't have planned it better myself.

GAMES ATTENDED, BY LOCATION: (through 5/19/97)

State or Province	# of Games	State or Province	# of Games
New York	999	Maryland	44
Minnesota	503	Michigan	44
Pennsylvania	301	Ontario	32
Illinois	266	Georgia	29
Massachusetts	216	Connecticut	27
California	181	Hawaii	26
Florida	168	Ohio	20
New Jersey	79	British Columbia	18
Missouri	70	Alberta	15
Quebec	58	14 other states, prov., & DC	84

GAME

Fenway Park **2847**

Chicago White Sox at Boston Red Sox

GAME

Boston Garden **2848**

Montreal Canadiens at Boston Bruins

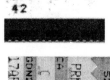

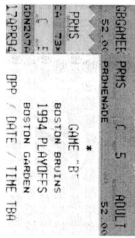

Patriots Day is still a great day to be in Boston; the Red Sox play at 11am; by the time the game ends and I walk back to my hotel at Copley Place, the streets are full of marathoners, most of them still on their hind legs, but some collapsed along Boylston Street, especially in the block beyond the finish line. Marathon running is another sport I've never gotten into, not as a spectator and certainly not as a participant; but the Marathon is an event that brings a festive atmosphere to an otherwise dreary spring day; I had plenty of time to get to the Garden for the Bruins playoff game; the Fleet Center is beginning to take shape immediately next door to the Garden so I know the days are numbered for this old favorite building. Unlike Chicago Stadium, which appears in excellent shape, the Garden is showing its age; I become more comfortable with the notion of a new arena in Boston when, seated in my rinkside seat about forty five minutes before face off a workman enters my section with a scooper, and captures a live rodent in the row two rows behind mine. Both Boston teams are beaten this day, but my most vivid memories are of the runners, humans in the downtown streets, and the rat trying to prolong his residence in the side promenade.

Chicago, April 24, 1994

GAME

2852  Chicago Stadium
New York Knickerbockers
at Chicago Bulls

GAME

2853  Comiskey Park
Detroit Tigers at Chicago White Sox

GAME

2854 Chicago Stadium
Toronto Maple Leafs
at Chicago Blackhawks

Three games in a day in Chicago once again; this time they all count; the Bulls and Knicks complete the NBA regular season in the regular season finale starting at noon; with a ticket to the ball game already in my pocket, I stay for the entire basketball game and arrive at Comiskey in the fourth inning; interestingly, quite a few others were also arriving, so I surmise that others took the opportunity for a Bulls-Sox doubleheader. And I'm sure that others besides myself were back at the Stadium for the Hawks-Leafs Stanley Cup playoff game that evening. The hockey game was the only one in which I had any real rooting interest, and the only victory for a Chicago team this day. The Blackhawks playoffs were especially important this year, since once they ended, I would never again see a hockey game in Chicago Stadium; the United Center would open across the street in the fall. So the Blackhawks 5-4 overtime victory, tying the series at two games apiece gave me hope that they would prevail over the Leafs in the opening round and extend the life of my favorite arena a few more weeks.

GAME

Chicago Stadium **2855**

Toronto Maple Leafs at Chicago Blackhawks

REMEMBER THE ROAR

CHICAGO BLACKHAWK
1994
STANLEY CUP
PLAYOFFS
DATE - TIME
TO BE ANNOUNCED

Sometimes in hockey, the offense stalls like a car with a dead battery; nothing will go in the net; when that happens in the playoffs, it normally signals an early summer; it was that excruciating type of week for the Hawks. The overtime winner of game four would be the team's last goal of the year; facing elimination in game six, they had dozens of scoring chances, right up to the final minute, but couldn't get even the one goal they would have needed to force overtime; a 1-0 Leafs victory ended the Hawks season, and, more importantly, marked the last hockey game ever played at Chicago Stadium. I lingered quite a while after the game, and then took the CTA express bus back to downtown, all the while looking out the back window until the historic old building disappeared from view for the last time.

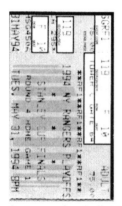

New York, May 31, 1994

GAME

Madison Square Garden **2857**

Vancouver Canucks at New York Rangers

Ranger fans have heard more than enough of the derisive chants of "1940!1940!", the constant reminder that it has been 54 years since the team's last Stanley Cup championship. This will be the year; the finals open at MSG with the usual boisterous, fanatic Ranger crowd on hand. Stories are told of the fans who have stayed loyal to their team throughout the 54 years; in fact, very few individuals at Ranger games in 1993-94 were part of the crowds in the early seventies, when I went to forty Rangers home games each year for three consecutive seasons; tonight, however, I noticed something different. At the first intermission, I walked over to Section 225, where I had sat for years, and noted one familiar face after another; several recognized me; we were all twenty years older than when we last saw each other, so identification was tentative at first; I cancelled my season tickets in 1976, but several of my neighbors in 225 had kept theirs, selling all but a very few of the games; one of them had moved away from New York years before and sold his tickets with the sole condition that he could use them in the Stanley Cup finals; for the first time in fifteen years, he was back in the seats; at the second intermission, I checked out Section 212 where my seats had been when the Garden opened in 1968; thankfully, no sign of Penn Bar. The debate in the Garden was not whether the Rangers would win the Cup, but whether they would lose one of the first four games, so the clincher could come in game five at the Garden; shortly into overtime; a Canucks goal stunned the Ranger crowd; suddenly it looked like a long road to the Cup.

Vancouver, June 11, 1994

GAME

2858 🏒 Pacific Coliseum

New York Rangers at Vancouver Canucks

Could this be the day the curse is overcome? The Rangers lead the Canucks three games to two in the Stanley Cup Finals; game six is set for 5pm in Vancouver. I board a Northwest flight to Vancouver that morning; if an event happens only once every fifty four years it's a good idea to show up when you have the chance. The flight looks like a charter for the Rangers fan club, loaded with passengers connecting from New York; during the flight, I make the acquaintance of two Wall Street traders who are flying out for the game; neither has ever been to Vancouver; I'm renting a car to drive back to Seattle for the red-eye flight home after the game, so I volunteer to drive them downtown and show them around Vancouver for the afternoon. By the time we got through customs, we met another New Yorker who had an extra ticket, just a few rows behind the Vancouver bench; so we were set to celebrate the first Rangers Stanley Cup victory of our lifetimes; my companions started celebrating a little early, several hours before the game in fact; these guys had Jet Pack potential. I'm sure they wore expensive suits to the office but today they were dressed like mannequins in the window of Cosby's Sporting Goods in the Garden lobby, head to toe Ranger gear; I was dressed normally, but my own affiliation was betrayed by one look at my three companions. Sadly, the game was a disappointment; the Canucks were in command the whole game and won 4-1, forcing a seventh game back in New York. I had until 1am to get to Seattle, so I drove my friends back downtown in my car; as we crawled through Vancouver traffic, our car, because of its three occupants in Ranger jerseys, became a target of unruly mobs that were forming along the sidewalks in Vancouver; we would have felt safer in the South Bronx; could I get away from the crowds and take some back streets to downtown? should I go to the American Embassy and seek asylum? Or, would we actually make it to downtown Vancouver alive? Fortunately, we made it safely to my friends' hotel; I dropped them off and headed south to Seattle without looking back. A business commitment in Chicago kept me from being in New York for game seven, so the Rangers won their only Cup without me. But I'll be there next time; I've marked my calendar for June, 2048.

Maui, November 23, 1994

GAME

Lahaina Civic Center 2877

Arizona State vs. Maryland

Without doubt, the annual pre-season Maui classic is the best kept secret in college basketball. Played in a gymnasium smaller than at most high schools, the tournament includes seven mainland teams, representing most of the top conferences from the ACC to the Pac 10. Four months hence, people will pay $1,000 a ticket to see some of these same teams from a far greater distance; here in Maui the most distant vantage point is ten bleacher rows from the court. Only a couple of thousand can fit into the gym, but the participating teams manage to find room for fans willing to make the trip. Since one can not reach Maui by bus or pick-up truck, the crowds are considerably more upscale than most, which is fine with me. Regrettably, however, even the Pacific Ocean fails to have a modulating impact on the behavior of fans representing states (Kansas and Kentucky come to mind), where little of consequence, besides basketball, has ever happened.

MOST FREQUENT GAME LOCATIONS:

Madison Square Garden (new) New York 342
Nassau Coliseum Long Island 260
Met Center Minneapolis 212
Metrodome Minneapolis..195
Core States Spectrum Philadelphia.....................................187
Chicago Stadium...153
Madison Square Garden (old) New York 141
Shea Stadium New York..129
Boston Garden 88
Target Center Minneapolis 80
Yankee Stadium New York 64
Great Western Forum Los Angeles 56
Fenway Park Boston 55

Chicago, January 25, 1995

GAME

2890  United Center

Edmonton Oilers at
Chicago Blackhawks

The lockout has ended and hockey starts its abbreviated forty game season; too bad there's not a lockout every year; avoid overlap with football and play few enough games so the regular season could be taken seriously. For the Hawks the season opens in the United Center, the huge new arena built across the street from the legendary Stadium, now in the process of being demolished. Changes from the Stadium are evident from the outset; as new buildings go, United Center is pretty good, and, for myself, I had no complaints about seating; my seats are in the last row downstairs, so whoever is immediately behind me is in a luxury box. Sixty dollars a ticket isn't cheap, but someone (more likely some corporation) right behind me put up a quarter million, so I can't complain about the location; others are not so fortunate; many of the long-time die hard Hawks fans who were so much a part of the noisy, flag-waving, devoted Stadium crowd have been banished, through seniority or affordability, to the upper reaches of United Center, altitudes which could turn an astronaut's stomach. The old Stadium was opened in 1929, and its seats were noticeably narrower than in most other buildings; the manufacturer must still be in business, because while the UC is modern in every respect, the seats are no wider; an overweight couple might be wise to consider three season tickets. Of course, it takes a cryptographer to determine which ticket, printed with dates from the original schedule, is valid for which game and date on the revised schedule; the opening game ticket looks more like a Christmas card than a game ticket, so many fans threw it away, adding to the opening night confusion.

Chicago, January 27, 1995

GAME

United Center 2891

Toronto Maple Leafs at Chicago Blackhawks

The Hawks second home game is two days later; a distinct change in the persona of the Hawk fan, at least in the lower level, more expensive sections, is becoming evident. To my right is a block of eight seats, obviously owned by a business with lots of customers, none of whom have ever seen a hockey game; the occupants of the seats constantly move in and out of the arena while play continues, and do so, maddeningly, one at a time so the flow of human traffic never stops; in the old Stadium the die hard fans would have put up the stop sign in no uncertain terms, but it does no good to talk to these people, because you never would be telling the same person more than once. I theorize that eleven people are sharing these eight seats. In front of me sits the "Perfect Hockey Family" of the nineties, happily being separated from their money with a velocity heretofore unknown in NHL history. $240 a night covers the four tickets, but Dad digs a lot deeper than that. Mom's new best friend is the Mai Tai vendor; by the second intermission she has lapsed into semi-consciousness; two young boys, dressed from head to toe in expensive official Hawks logo clothing complete the Perfect Hockey Family. Of course, the boys hardly ever watch the game; they return from the concession stands intermittently to get more cash from Dad. A nice family, well behaved, courteous, and friendly; but as I'll learn over the next couple of seasons, not the most astute hockey observers in town.

Minneapolis, February 18, 1995

GAME

Williams Arena 2894

Michigan State vs. Minnesota

It's the toughest ticket in Minneapolis and rightfully so; the "Old Barn" jams more fans into less cubic footage than any building I can think of. In this intimate atmosphere, every Big 10 game is a great show; many of the regulars were in college even longer ago than me; the Barn is the one of few places where I don't feel like one of the oldest spectators. As in most big time college arenas, rationality is checked at the door; fans dress in maroon and gold and obediently chant, cheer and sing as instructed by the cheerleaders, dance team, band and, mascot Goldy Gopher, a friendly rodent far less offensive than most of his counterparts. There is a seriousness about the game that reminds me of some of the Canadian hockey followers; the coach's every move is analyzed and, if the team fails to win, second guessed; even after all my years in Minnesota I can't begin to take the Gophers nearly as seriously as the natives do, but I nevertheless find every game at the Barn most enjoyable.

Boston, May 8, 1995

GAME

2912 Boston Garden

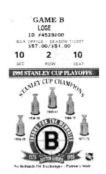

New Jersey Devils at Boston Bruins

The 1995 NHL season was most unusual in that Eastern and Western teams did not play each other, so the only interconference games would be the Stanley Cup finals. In the West, Detroit seemed to be the logical pick for the finals, and most observers felt the Wings would win the Cup, since the East did not have a single dominant team. I felt the overall level of play was considerably higher in the East this season, but absent interconference games, that was tough to verify. This night my attention was focused on the building; it would be the last game the Bruins would play in their legendary home; while my attention was on the building, I gradually became aware of the complete dominance of the Devils; they shut out the Bruins 3-0 with their aggressive forechecking style (which became known as "the trap"); the trap became so frustrating to other teams that a casual observer might have thought it to be illegal; I found it fascinating as the Devils denied opponents the skating space and momentum needed to take advantage of their scoring potential. In the third period, I concluded that this Devils team was playing the best defensive hockey I had ever seen; I realized that Western Conference teams did not play this way for the most part, and would have great difficulty with the Devils should New Jersey get to the finals.

Detroit, June 20, 1995

GAME

2922 Joe Louis Arena

New Jersey Devils at Detroit Red Wings

The Red Wings were upset by the Devils in game one of the finals at Detroit; but one game does not decide a Cup; after all, last year the Rangers were beaten in the first game at home and went on to win the Cup; the majority of forecasters felt that the Wings would capture their first Cup since 1955; but the Wings loss in game one was no surprise to me, and I expected no different tonight. In fact, so sure was I of the outcome of this series that I left voicemails for two friends before the finals, predicting a Devils sweep to the Cup in four straight games; regrettably, neither of my friends is a bookie. The Wings fans are nervous outside the Joe on this summer night, but the octopus stand was still doing a brisk business; the most bizarre tradition in all of sports, throwing live (or are they dead) octopi on the Detroit ice, has taken hold in a big way this year. I don't so much mind the deluge during the anthem, but where have those octopi thrown in the third period been for the last several hours? Pickpockets have learned to steer clear of this crowd! The Wings crowd gets increasingly nervous as the game goes on; the trap continues to be highly effective, and a 4-2 Devils victory seals the Wings fate. I leave the arena confident in my forecasting ability, and two games later, when the Devils complete their sweep, I leave a couple of I told you so voicemails.

Tiger Stadium ⚾ 2930

Oakland Athletics at Detroit Tigers

Bad weather has kept me from games from time to time, but this was the first time bad weather took me to a game I had not planned to attend; Heavy thunderstorms hit Detroit just after my flight landed in late afternoon; driving toward my hotel north of downtown the heavy rain made driving very difficult and dangerous; radio reports said that conditions were even worse in the Troy area where I was headed, and that some freeways there were under water. I needed a place to wait out the storm; I was at a freeway exit near Tiger Stadium; I thought I would go there, with little expectation that tonight's scheduled game would be played, buy a ticket and sit under cover in the old ball park until the rain subsided. The corner of Michigan and Trumbull is not normally a place sought out for personal safety, but that was exactly my reason for heading there this night. To my surprise the storm stopped, the sun came out, the Athletics and Tigers skipped batting practice but played a ball game. By the time I got to my hotel around eleven this night, the storm was just a memory, and I had added an unscheduled game to my sports journey.

Pontiac Silverdome 🏈 2941

San Francisco 49ers at Detroit Lions

The 49ers have been my favorites since my days at Kezar thirty years ago; and I've seen them more frequently on Monday night than any other team, usually on the road; this will be the first time I've seen them play the Lions, although the Silverdome is where I saw the 49ers win their first Super Bowl. The Silverdome doesn't sell out very often, not even for the several Thanksgiving Day games I attended in the late eighties; but this crowd was as fired up as any in the NFL; the Dome was full and the Lions, off to their accustomed slow early season start were in late season form; a tie at the end of regulation didn't worry me; I'd seen more than my share of 49er late game comebacks and last second victories; but in overtime the Lions prevail, 27-24; I was only slightly disappointed; I've seen a great football game and that's more important to me than whether or not my team wins.

Denver, October 9, 1995

GAME

2947  McNichols Arena

Pittsburgh Penguins at Colorado Avalanche

It is the second home game for the Colorado Avalanche, newly arrived from Quebec; this early in the season, few were giving any thought to the Stanley Cup which would reside in Denver the following summer; in fact, most of the folks outside Big Mac before this game were desperately trying to unload game tickets at a fraction of what they originally cost; I thought this was amazing, inasmuch as it was the Penguins only visit of the year, and, only the second home game for the franchise. The novelty factor alone should have created high ticket demand. It had been over fifteen years since my last game in this building, before the Colorado Rockies moved to New Jersey; how our standards and expectations of arenas have changed; I recalled this building as new, clean, attractive and comfortable; tonight it seemed like an aging dump, way below NHL standards.

Chicago, October 12, 1995

GAME

2948  United Center

Pittsburgh Penguins at Chicago Blackhawks

Opening night of the new hockey season. It's going to be a long one; last year's truncated forty game regular season and the Devils playoff dominance was just about right; now three extra months of only occasionally intense games are added; without the electric atmosphere of the Stadium, now reincarnated as Premium Parking, twice weekly trips to Chicago are going to become a burden. The Perfect Hockey Family is back for another year; shortly after the first period starts, Dad turns and asks: "By the way, who won the Stanley Cup last year?" $240 a game into Hawks tickets and he doesn't know! Actually if he was truly the perfect Hawks fan, he would have been bamboozled into believing that the video of the 1961 Hawks championship which is shown ad nauseam on the big screen before each game really took place last spring, not thirty four long years ago. Shortly after I reveal that the Devils are Stanley Cup champions, Perfect Hockey Mom demands a cellular phone; is she calling the mai tai vendor? No, her sister is at the game, on the other side of the building, and they need to chat, woman to woman, cell phone to cell phone. With this devoted a following, the Hawks are a lock for this year's Stanley Cup.

DENVER
VS.
LOS ANGELES
MON., OCT. 16, 1995 · 7:00 PM
DENVER MILE HIGH STADIUM

THIRD LEVEL

339	12	7
SEC	ROW	SEAT

Denver, October 16, 1995

GAME

Mile High Stadium  2949

Oakland Raiders at Denver Broncos

For all the NFL games I've attended, there are still a couple of spots on the NFL circuit which I've never visited; apart from the new stadiums and new franchises, the only NFL home teams I'd missed were Green Bay, Buffalo and Denver; therefore, I welcomed to opportunity to work with a client in Colorado who set up a meeting that coincided with Monday Night Football at Mile High. Oakland and Denver is one of the storied rivalries in football, and while far more subdued than a generation ago, still usually an intense battle. But there is a mystique about Monday night that brings out the best in the home teams (ask any handicapper), and tonight, that mystique, combined with the fact that the Broncos needed the win more than Oakland, carried the Broncos to a 27-0 victory. My seat was good, the weather perfect, and the stadium, though old and multi-tiered, surprisingly attractive and comfortable.

Mon., Oct. 30, 1995-8:00
HHH METRODOME

ACCT. NO. **5-16483**

F	132	6	20
GATE	SEC.	ROW	SEAT

Minneapolis, October 30, 1995

GAME

Metrodome 2952

Chicago Bears at Minnesota Vikings

I hardly ever miss a Vikings game, but hardly ever remember much about the games either; on Sundays, I'm often tempted to leave at half-time to watch six other NFL games simultaneously in my living room; but the annual Monday night game is always a big event; this night was one to be remembered, but not for what happened in the game; after all, the Vikings have followed the same script for years: beat nearly everyone at home during the season, lose during the playoffs, and play disappointing football on the road. My seats at the Dome are directly behind the visitors bench, six rows up from the field; while I'm normally not sympathetic to fans who shout at players, there is one exception, Darren, a very creative young man behind me who harasses, in an entertaining way, visiting players most nights; this night being close to Halloween, many fans came in costume; accompanying Darren this night was a friend wearing a skin colored body suit, decorated to appear to be a naked woman, anatomically correct in every detail. Of course, from a distance of, say fifty feet, it was easy to tell this was a costume; but for fifty thousand other spectators, and the ABC cameras, it looked like the real thing; this pair entertained the fans, and the Bears players, this night; a 14-6 Bears victory wouldn't normally be called a "laugher", but it was for all Bears players who turned their back to the field for even a moment.

New York,   December 13, 1995

GAME

2971 Madison Square Garden

Boston Bruins at
New York Rangers

R angers fans are an eclectic mix of rogues and scoundrels, laborers and entrepreneurs, auto mechanics and stock brokers; dressed in jeans and T-shirts or thousand dollar suits, they are unified by their allegiance to their team. It is a myth that the only true Ranger fans are in the cheap seats, and that the expensive "red" and "orange" levels are occupied by the idle rich, indifferent to hockey and taking up space coveted by the more ardent, but less affluent sectors of the Rangers constituency. True, there aren't many suits in the blue seats, and sometimes the pricey seats are occupied by know-nothings paying no attention to the game, paying nothing for their seats, and discussing the petty politics of their profession for all three periods; true Rangers fans, of all social strata, are rightfully resentful of these interlopers; on this night, I'm invited to a business dinner and the game by a colleague; his two other guests are attending their first game ever. We meet for dinner, so naturally we arrive late, well into the first period, four suits heading for our choice corporate seats; the two neophytes, more to be polite than anything, asked some rudimentary questions about the game but the conversation quickly moved deeply into the issues of mutual interest in our consulting engagements; I barely could remember it was the Bruins and Rangers, and really did not feel in touch with the game, even though our seats were among the best in the Garden. In the third period, I experienced a moment of terror: I am living my own worst nightmare, using prime seats paid for with corporate funds as a conference room; Section 225 was right behind us; carefully I looked around; I hope there's no one here who will recognize me; I'd be so embarrassed. I've attended lots of games with business associates, but never tried to force hockey on someone who was unfamiliar with the sport; I'd much rather go to a game alone than with someone whose love and understanding of the sport is so much less than my own.

San Francisco,   December 18, 1995

GAME

3Com Park 2973

Minnesota Vikings at San Francisco 49ers

Where better to spend my fifty fifth birthday than in my favorite city as my first favorite team hosts my current local team; one of Jerry's sons cooperates by getting ill, so space is available with his regular, long-time fellow 49er fanatics. I wanted pictures to commemorate the occasion; Jerry correctly pointed out that we would have to find among the nearby fans one who was both sober enough to operate the camera, but honest enough not to steal it, a difficult parlay among 49er fans, particularly in the second half; we selected a volunteer to take several photos; our parlay did not pay off; no pictures, but at least I got my camera back.

Montreal,   January 10, 1996

GAME

Montreal Forum   2979

Vancouver Canucks at
Montreal Canadiens

Once again, I say farewell to a beloved hockey building. The Montreal Forum is to be replaced by a bigger, higher revenue version, with the Molson Centre due to open in just a few weeks; I knew I would not return to Montreal in the Forum's remaining lifetime, so this was a very special visit; I spent much of the time trying to figure out what exactly was wrong with the Forum that required replacement. The answer is nothing. The old Forum had outstanding sight lines, and a fair number of luxury boxes; Canadiens games are always sold out, with long lines at the Molson taps before games and during intermissions. Seated just three rows behind the goal, I enjoyed the 2-2 Canadiens-Canucks tie immensely; compared to years ago, more French and less English is spoken in the prime seats; otherwise the Forum was the same temple of hockey it had always been. The decline of Montreal is now complete; a quarter century ago, I couldn't go there frequently enough; now some of the familiar stores and restaurants are closed or gone, much of the city is in disrepair, many businesses have left the Province and now, worst of all, there's no Montreal Forum. I stayed ten minutes after the game, took a couple of photos of the now empty Forum and left.

Dunedin, March 2, 1996

GAME

2993 Dunedin Stadium

Philadelphia Phillies at Toronto Blue Jays

Tampa, March 2, 1996

GAME

2994 The Sun Dome

Alabama Birmingham at U S F

I t is easier to find a Canadian citizen poolside at my condo than at the wheel of a Toronto taxicab these days. A few years ago there was a solemn daily caravan to Blue Jays spring training games; more recently snowbirds have jumped off the bandwagon faster than Blue Jay free agents jumping for American dollars. Dunedin Stadium is nearly empty as the Phils and Blue Jays, thirty months ago World Series opponents, square off preparing for what promises to be a dismal season for both. Times are tough for the Labatt's vendors at the ball park, but at least they are less hassled by customers who actually haggle over the price of a beer; more and more nowadays, the vendors are actually able to collect American currency at the ball park, so the end of the Blue Jay glory days is not a complete disaster. Following the game I head to Tampa for the best-kept sports secret in the Tampa Bay area; on the campus of the University of South Florida in the beautiful Sun Dome, Conference USA basketball, featuring big-time powers such as Tulane, Cincinnati, and Memphis visit to play the South Florida Bulls. UAB and USF are not tournament teams this year, but the game is a high quality Division I matchup, played in a simple yet highly functional building. No high pressure commercialism, no lame animal mascots, hardly a concession stand to be found; at half time, the USF homecoming king and queen are crowned; the crowd is well behaved, many wearing the green sport jackets reserved for USF's more significant benefactors.

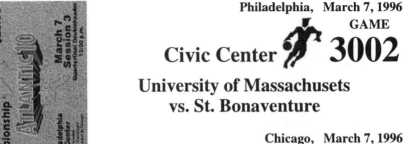

Philadelphia, March 7, 1996
GAME
Civic Center 3002
University of Massachusets
vs. St. Bonaventure

Chicago, March 7, 1996
GAME
United Center 3003
Detroit Pistons at Chicago Bulls

I passed the three thousand game mark in Philadelphia, shuttling in cold rain between the Palestra, the Spectrum and Convention Hall. The Atlantic 10 tournament was continuing all week, but I was anxious to get out of town, especially when the forecast was for the rain to turn to an ice storm by Thursday afternoon. I skipped the second game of the afternoon doubleheader and moved my Chicago flight ahead from 7pm to 3pm; as a result I arrived in Chicago by 5pm. Talk about turning adversity into opportunity; I was in Chicago in time for the Bulls-Pistons game, sitting about twelve rows up behind the Bulls bench; in the second half, Michael Jordan took the game into his own hands, scoring fifty-three points to lead the Bulls to an easy victory. But for the ice storm I would have been at another A-10 match in a near-empty arena.

 FAVORITE BASKETBALL ARENAS:

Pro:

1. Madison Square Garden, New York
2. Great Western Forum, Los Angeles
3. Target Center, Minneapolis
4. America West Arena, Phoenix
5. United Center, Chicago

College:

1. The Palestra, Philadelphia
2. Sun Dome, Tampa
3. Lahaina Civic Center, Maui
4. Williams Arena, Minnesota
5. Greensboro Coliseum, ACC

Greensboro, March 8, 1996

GAME

3004 Greensboro Coliseum

Maryland vs. Duke

GAME

3005 Greensboro Coliseum

North Carolina State vs. Georgia Tech

Chicago, March 8, 1996

GAME

3006  United Center

Los Angeles Kings at Chicago Blackhawks

The ACC tournament is an annual Woodstock-like festival for its nine Eastern schools and their basketball-intense followers; you have to be there to believe it; the parking lot is loaded hours before game time; even on this unusually cold Carolina morning, all nine teams are well represented; at least six of the nine teams are within easy driving distance of Greensboro, the other three no more than a half day away; the license plates and banners confirm that the crowd is roughly equally divided nine ways; so is the arena, as the oldest and/or most generous alums get prime lower level seats, with the same school colors worn by others in that ninth of the building all the way to the top; a fortune could be made in the parking lots; tons of people are looking for tickets, but plenty are for sale; I buy an upper for insurance, then trade up to a good lower among Clemson supporters; actually, for early rounds, just being in the building is sufficient for empty seats are available, if not plentiful, in the seven ninths of the building dedicated to the seven teams not playing at the moment; even inside the building fans carry "I need tickets" signs, since there are three more doubleheaders to be played before the annual festival closes down on Sunday. Following the afternoon doubleheader, I returned to the airport for my return flight to O'Hare; much as I would have liked to stay for the evening doubleheader, I wanted to see the Blackhawks game as well; such is the subtle pressure of season tickets; over time, one goes to more games than they otherwise would, and, much as I love hockey, this was a Hawks game I might have skipped. For the fourth time in eight days I flew into Chicago for a game at United Center; it was one of the great sports travel weeks of my entire journey.

vs. NEW YORK
KNICKS
$82.00 Tax Included

GAME

Target Center 3007

New York Knickerbockers at Minnesota Timberwolves

Throw a net over the courtside sections at Target Center and one could capture the highest concentration of native New Yorkers ever to congregate in Minneapolis. This is especially true when the Knicks visit, but all year long the courtside locations are coveted by those who, like myself, know that pro basketball is best enjoyed from the front rows and that the Wolves $82 price is by far the best value in the NBA; if this game were in the Garden, these seats would cost $1,000 and not exactly available to the public at any price. Last time I looked NBA teams use the same roster in road games as at home, so the best show in the NBA is most readily available in my home city; and the Timberwolves roster is improving rapidly; within a couple of years, assuming players are not lost to free agency, the Wolves should be near the top of the NBA; of course, there could be some wishful thinking in that prediction; when $7,000 toward the team's salary cap appears on your Visa statement, it stimulates partisan interest in the team's success.

SEASON TICKET HOLDINGS:

Current:	# of Years	Previous:	# of Years
Washington Redskins	27	New York Rangers	13
Miami Dolphins	13	Minnesota North Stars	7
Tampa Bay Buccaneers	13	New York Knickerbockers	6
Minnesota Vikings	11	Philadelphia Flyers	6
New York Jets	8	New York Islanders	5
Chicago Blackhawks	7	Philadelphia 76ers	3
Philadelphia Phillies (spring training)	5	San Francisco 49ers	2
Minnesota Timberwolves	3	Tampa Bay Lightning	1

Indianapolis, March 14, 1996

GAME

3008 RCA Dome

Eastern Michigan vs. Duke

GAME

3009 RCA Dome

Mississippi State vs.
Virginia Commonwealth

GAME

3010 RCA Dome

U C L A vs. Princeton

F ew would dispute that, on average, Princeton students would be favored in an intellectual match over most other collegians, including those at U C L A; but whatever that IQ or SAT point differential might be, Princeton more than covered the spread in the RCA Dome tonight; Princeton's defeat of defending national champion UCLA was the biggest upset I've ever attended; the Jets upset of the Colts in Super Bowl III doesn't compare; at least a handful of the Jets would have made the Colts roster, and all the Jets would have been allowed to come to tryouts. Conversely, not one member of the Princeton team could have made the UCLA roster as a walk-on. Princeton's team, athletes without scholarships, out-thought the vastly more talented UCLA roster; coach Pete Carril, about to retire from college coaching, prepared a game plan that slowed the tempo to a walk and limited the shots available to either team; Princeton fell behind by as much as ten points early in the game, but stuck to the game plan; the clock struck midnight in Indianapolis, the game was ending with Princeton 43-41 victors. A long day of basketball, with the final game far overshadowing the earlier two.

Jack Russell Stadium ⚾ 3015

Texas Rangers at Philadelphia Phillies

It's my favorite place in all of Florida. Welcome to a time warp; the intimate little ballpark has hardly changed in the half century it has been the spring home of the Phillies; local merchants' ads cover the outfield walls; the scoreboard has been electrified, but one would almost expect a message to flash: JAPANESE SURRENDER, WAR IS OVER! An octogenarian organist sits among the crowd, with a tips jar beside the organ; my seats are nine rows above the Phillies dugout, in a section frequently occupied by Phils family, executives and former players. The fans, for the most part, are like the ball park, old but still very much in the game. No matter that the pitchers can't pitch, the fielders can't field and the very act of donning the red and white pinstripes is Philly's greatest health risk since Legionnaire's Disease, this ball park is a delightful reminder of the franchise's glorious past, with just a hint of its dubious future.

Chicago, April 19, 1996

GAME

3032  Wrigley Field

San Francisco Giants at Chicago Cubs

GAME

3033 United Center

Calgary Flames at Chicago Blackhawks

I f dressed for the weather, it's a great time to be in Chicago; the Cubs and Sox are starting their season, the Bulls and Hawks have moved on to the playoffs. It is brutally cold and windy at Wrigley Field, but it is still Wrigley Field; I take advantage of the sparsity of the crowd and try to keep warm by moving to a different seat location every couple of innings; for the first time in over thirty years, I sit in the upper deck for awhile, right above first base; it's even colder than my seat just above the Giants dugout, but it does afford a good, albeit more distant than I prefer, panoramic view of this great baseball shrine. In the evening, I'm off to United Center; the Hawks hopes are high for the playoffs despite some formidable competition in the Western Conference from Colorado and Detroit; I'm pleased that Calgary is the first round opponent, because I think the Hawks match up well and should have little trouble advancing at least to the Conference semi-finals. The Perfect Hockey Family is on hand, of course, their tab now up to $360 per game, plus parking and mai tais. They decide on an early exit to beat traffic. Perfect Hockey Dad, ever the gentleman, bids goodbye to his neighbor: "We're leaving now. Good night. See you in the playoffs". A minute and a half later the game ends and the Blackhawks take a two games to none lead in this year's opening playoff round.

Q *UESTION FREQUENTLY ASKED OF THE AUTHOR:*

Do you have to be wealthy to be a sports traveler?

Absolutely not! It certainly helps to have a job requiring travel to big league cities, but even that is not necessary. Even at today's inflated ticket prices, my annual net cost for tickets and travel is in the $10 to $15 thousand range; compared to my friends with golf addictions, my habit is relatively inexpensive to feed.

GAME

United Center 🏒 **3037**

Colorado Avalanche
at Chicago Blackhawks

I hate overtime, especially the extra five minutes the NHL adds to tied regular season games; if two teams play evenly for sixty minutes, then each deserves a point in the standings, and shouldn't gain or lose a point based on what is all too often a fluke, a lucky bounce, an errant pass, in extra time; Stanley Cup playoff games have always been settled by sudden death overtime, a necessary evil since the series must be decided one way or the other; playoff overtime matches are usually characterized by effective, defensive-minded play, and good officiating; if a penalty is called in overtime, it is by all means deserved; no team will be given a power play unless they have been victimized by a serious foul. Some of the best hockey all season is played in the sudden death periods; this year the Hawks are playing more than their share; tonight they lose in the second overtime; another game in this series went three overtimes; great hockey, but the kitchens are closed where I normally have my post-game meal. Given the length of three period games, which often approach three hours in duration, I prefer to see overtime settled quickly. But the three overtime games in this series were all close checking, with scoring opportunities very limited; some fans were more inconvenienced than others; the beer stands close in the third period; by a second overtime this is a serious problem for some fans; one friend of mine was able to get refills from a private club near our seats; when the game ended fans stampeded toward the exits, nearly trampling my friend who was on his way into the seating area; hoisting two beers proudly, he asked me: Where's everyone going? He'd forgotten it was sudden death overtime many beers ago.

QUESTION FREQUENTLY ASKED OF THE AUTHOR:

What places you've never gone do you still want to visit?

Notre Dame Stadium and Green Bay's Lambeau Field are the two that come immediately to mind. The NBA and NHL are building new arenas faster than I can keep up, so there are several stops to be made there as well; finally, my long hiatus from college basketball leaves dozens of fascinating venues yet to be explored; the journey is far from over.

Detroit, May 19, 1996

GAME

3038 Joe Louis Arena

Colorado Avalanche at Detroit Red Wings

Detroit, May 19, 1996

GAME

3039  Tiger Stadium

Chicago White Sox at Detroit Tigers

It was a beautiful spring Sunday in Hockeytown USA as the Western Conference finals began; the Wings were shocked last year by the Devils in the Stanley Cup finals; this year the path to the Cup looks clearer; the immediate obstacle is the Avalanche, a team which until this year were the Quebec Nordiques. Mike Keane's overtime goal for Colorado sent the Wings fans home disappointed; I was not disappointed, nor was I going home; ten minutes after Keane's goal I pulled into a parking lot across from Tiger Stadium; a beautiful night for a ball game in a nearly empty park. Unlike many of the new stadiums with extensive foul territory, the first rows of seats at Tiger Stadium are very close to home plate; seated in the third row just to the right of the plate, I felt very much "in the game"; after eight hours of Detroit sports and a good night's sleep, it's off to Pittsburgh for more Stanley Cup playoff action.

MOST MEMORABLE GAMES:

Hockey: April 29, 1971
Rangers defeat Hawks on Pete Stemkowski's goal in the third sudden death overtime period

Baseball: August 15, 1990
Terry Mulholland of Phillies no-hits Giants at the Vet

Football: January 27, 1991
Giants beat Bills in Super Bowl XXV as Scott Norwood misses last second field goal

Basketball: March 14, 1996
Princeton upsets defending national champion UCLA in NCAA tournament

GAME

Metrodome 🏈 3041

California Angels at Minnesota Twins

The Twins are baseball's most overachieving and underappreciated team; year in and year out, they play sound fundamental baseball and win more games than handicappers would forecast based on talent alone. Except for the occasional pennant run, the Twins are largely ignored by local fans; of course, there's not much appeal to spending a beautiful summer day watching baseball in a domed football stadium; this night the Dome is even emptier than usual, fewer than ten thousand fans on hand. When the Yankees, Red Sox, Indians or White Sox visit the crowds are enlarged by visiting team followers; but tonight's visitor is the Angels, who, by my theory, have no fans; that theory could not be disproved tonight. Baseball is a wonderful game because at every game something unique or at least highly unusual can happen; this game was more interesting than most because the Twins batted fourteen players in the fourth inning and scored nine runs enroute to an easy victory. In a few years, baseball will be even more interesting in my home city when the Twins get a legitimate outdoor baseball stadium like the ones in Baltimore, Cleveland and Denver; of course there are those who would let Twins move away, rather than provide subsidies and tax incentives to finance a new stadium. It's a safe bet none of those skeptics grew up in Brooklyn. Ideological arguments on the legitimacy of using public funds to subsidize professional sports are interesting, sometimes even compelling, but irrelevant. The Twins deserve a major league stadium; if Minnesota doesn't provide it, other places will; that is as true in 1997 as in 1957; all my NHL games are already road games; I would hate to see the same thing happen in baseball and watch my adopted home area gradually fade from the sports map. Did I move to Minnesota for sports? Of course not, it was strictly a business transfer; but I could have moved elsewhere; my love for Minnesota had been nurtured over the years by my many business trips, scheduled to coincide with Twins and North Stars games. I moved away from an area with more major league franchises within a four hour drive than occupy the entire Central Time Zone; I've paid more property and income taxes to the state than I would prefer, but do so willingly because of all the attractions, including major league sports; economists claim that pro sports franchises do not directly attract more revenue to a community; however, they can not quantify the impact of the indirect attraction; would I have spent a dollar of property, sales or income tax in Minnesota if I had moved to, say, Des Moines, Omaha, Indianapolis or Memphis? And without Minnesota's pro sports teams, how would I have known the difference?

San Francisco, July 18, 1996

GAME

3048  3Com Park

Los Angeles Dodgers
at San Francisco Giants

M y Angels have no fans theory withstood a strong test; I'm watching the Dodgers and Giants, the bitter rivals of my youth, battle each other at the park previously known as Candlestick. Dressed in clothes I'd wear outdoors in the Minnesota winter, I was quite comfortable; I was seated next to a rabid baseball fan, a woman who not long ago graduated from Long Beach State; surely, in four years in Southern California this very avid sportswoman would have met an Angel fan if any existed. So as not to bias her answer, I mentioned no team but asked if she could think of one well established major league team that has no fans. It took her about an inning and a half of concentrated thought; then her eyes lit up as she answered decisively: "Of course, the Angels." Case closed.

The 50th anniversary of my first game: July 25, 1996

GAME

Metrodome ⚾ 3052

Boston Red Sox at Minnesota Twins

The day has come! Fifty years ago today my Dad and I went to Ebbets Field for my first sporting event. Driving to the Metrodome this night, I reflect on the half century, and particularly how my Dad would react to tonight's game were he still alive to share our "anniversary". (Too bad the Dodgers and Cubs aren't playing each other tonight, so I could see the same match-up as fifty years ago). The Metrodome will have to do for the anniversary celebration. Dad would find it familiar to park in a city and walk to the stadium, although he would have marveled at the number of on-street parking spots available (at a quarter per half hour) within two blocks of the Dome. Once inside, Dad would have been bewildered by a number of things; first, the artificial surface and the resulting high bounces of the baseball, as though the game were being played in our concrete driveway back in Brooklyn. Looking up he would see a bizarre covering to the building, off white in color with lights and white patches that look like baseballs; he certainly couldn't follow any fly balls against that background; he'd blame failing eyesight, but for no reason; outfielders on both teams will let routine fly balls drop for hits in the first three innings. Dad would be interested in Tim Wakefield, the Red Sox knuckle-baller, and begin telling stories about Dutch Leonard and Jim Bagby; he wouldn't even have reached the Hoyt Wilhelm stories by the time the Twins figure out the knuckle ball and post a seven run fourth inning. We would have a good time, and stay about two and a half hours, just like fifty years ago. This time we wouldn't leave by walking across the outfield; even if that practice hadn't been discontinued decades ago, we couldn't walk across the field since only six innings are played in two and a half hours most games these days. No longer could we check a scoreboard with out-of-town results posted inning by inning in hand mounted letters and numbers; in its place would be an electronic message board constantly flashing commercials, cartoons, silly games (Dad would definitely not understand the "Great Tire Race") and every now and then the score of another game. But if we watched carefully enough, we'd see one message we could relate to, the announcement of the upcoming Twins schedule. I'd read it and say: "Boston here tomorrow, Dad, let's come again". And we probably would.

Appendix

Stadiums and

Arenas Visited

Stadiums and Arenas Visited

Location	Current Name	Previous Name(s)
Alberta		
Calgary	Canadian Airlines Saddledome	Olympic Saddledome
Calgary	Stampede Corral	
Edmonton	Edmonton Coliseum	Northlands Coliseum
Arizona		
Phoenix	America West Arena	
Phoenix	Municipal Stadium	
Scottsdale	Scottsdale Stadium	
Australia		
Melbourne	North Melbourne Oval	
British Columbia		
Vancouver	Pacific Coliseum	
California		
Anaheim	Anaheim Stadium	
Anaheim	Arrowhead Pond	
Los Angeles	Dodger Stadium	Chavez Ravine
Los Angeles	Great Western Forum	The Forum
Los Angeles	Los Angeles Memorial Coliseum	
Los Angeles	Los Angeles Sports Arena	
Oakland	Oakland-Alameda County Coliseum	
Oakland	Oakland Coliseum Arena	
Palm Springs	Angels Stadium	
Pasadena	Rose Bowl	
Sacramento	Arco Arena	
San Diego	Balboa Stadium	
San Diego	Qualcomm Stadium	Jack Murphy Stadium, San Diego Stadium
San Diego	San Diego Sports Arena	
San Francisco	3Com Park	Candlestick Park
San Francisco	Civic Auditorium	
San Francisco	Cow Palace	
San Francisco	Kezar Stadium	
San Jose	San Jose Arena	

Stadiums and Arenas Visited

Location	Current Name	Previous Name(s)
Colorado		
Denver	Mc Nichols Arena	
Denver	Mile High Stadium	
Connecticut		
Hartford	Civic Center Coliseum	
Hartford	Jessee Field	
Middletown	Alumni Field House	
Middletown	Andrus Field	
New Haven	Yale Bowl	
District of Columbia		
Washington	Griffith Stadium	
Washington	RFK Stadium	D.C. Stadium
Florida		
Bradenton	Mc Kechnie Field	
Clearwater	Jack Russell Stadium	
Dunedin	Dunedin Stadium	Grant Field
Fort Lauderdale	Lockhart Stadium	
Fort Lauderdale	Fort Lauderdale Stadium	Yankee Stadium
Miami	Miami Arena	
Miami	Orange Bowl	
Miami	Pro Player Park	Joe Robbie Stadium
Orlando	Orlando Arena	
Orlando	Citrus Bowl	
Orlando	Tinker Field	
Plant City	Plant City Stadium	
Sarasota	Ed Smith Stadium	
St. Petersburg	Al Lang Field	
St. Petersburg	Al Lang Stadium	
St. Petersburg	Campbell Park	
St. Petersburg	Tropicana Field	Thunderdome
Tampa	Al Lopez Field	
Tampa	Expo Hall	
Tampa	Houlihan's Stadium	Tampa Stadium
Tampa	Ice Palace	
Tampa	Legends Field	
Tampa	Sun Dome	
Vero Beach	Holman Stadium	
Winter Haven	Chain o' Lakes Park	

Stadiums and Arenas Visited

Location	Current Name	Previous Name(s)
Georgia		
Atlanta	Atlanta Fulton County Stadium	
Atlanta	The Omni	
Hawaii		
Honolulu	Aloha Stadium	
Lahania	Lahaina Civic Center	
Illinois		
Chicago	Chicago Stadium	
Chicago	Comiskey Park (new)	
Chicago	Comiskey Park (old)	
Chicago	Soldier Field	
Chicago	UIC Pavillion	
Chicago	United Center	
Chicago	Wrigley Field	
Evanston	Dyche Stadium	
Indiana		
Evansville	Roberts Coliseum	
Indianapolis	RCA Dome	Hoosier Dome
Indianapolis	Market Square Arena	
Lafayette	Ross-Ade Stadium	
Louisiana		
New Orleans	Louisiana Superdome	
Maine		
Waterville	Seavern Field	
Manitoba		
Winnipeg	Winnipeg Arena	
Maryland		
Annapolis	Navy-Marine Corps Stadium	
Baltimore	Civic Center	
Baltimore	Memorial Stadium	
Baltimore	Oriole Park	
Landover	US Air Arena	Capital Centre

Stadiums and Arenas Visited

Location	Current Name	Previous Name(s)
Massachusetts		
Amherst	Amherst Cage	
Amherst	Orr Rink	
Amherst	Pratt Field	
Boston	Boston Garden	
Boston	Fenway Park	
Boston	Nickerson Field	Braves Field
Foxboro	Foxboro Stadium	Schafer Stadium
		Sullivan Stadium
Medford	Tufts Oval	
Springfield	Blake Arena	
Springfield	Eastern States Coliseum	
Springfield	Springfield Civic Center	
Williamstown	Lansing Chapman Rink	
Williamstown	Lasell Gym	
Williamstown	Weston Field	
Michigan		
Auburn Hills	Palace of Auburn Hills	
Detroit	Joe Louis Arena	
Detroit	Olympia Stadium	
Detroit	Tiger Stadium	
Pontiac	Pontiac Silverdome	
Minnesota		
Bloomington	Metropolitan Sports Center	
Bloomington	Metropoltian Stadium	
Minneapolis	Mariucci Arena (old)	
Minneapolis	Mariucci Arena (new)	
Minneapolis	Metrodome	
Minneapolis	Target Center	
Minneapolis	Williams Arena	
St. Paul	St. Paul Civic Center	
St. Paul	Midway Stadium	

Stadiums and Arenas Visited

Location	Current Name	Previous Name(s)
Missouri		
Kansas City	Arrowhead Stadium	
Kansas City	Kemper Arena	
Kansas City	Municipal Stadium	
Kansas City	Royals Stadium	
St. Louis	Busch Stadium (old)	
St. Louis	Busch Stadium (new)	
St. Louis	Kiel Center	
St. Louis	St. Louis Arena	Checkerdome
New Jersey		
Cherry Hill	Cherry Hill Arena	
East Rutherford	Giants Stadium	
East Rutherford	Meadowlands Arena	Brendan Byrne Arena
Princeton	Palmer Stadium	
New York		
Brooklyn	Ebbets Field	
Brooklyn	Roosevelt Hall Gym	
Brooklyn	Fort Hamilton Arena	
Buffalo	Memorial Auditorium	
Flushing	National Tennis Center	
Flushing	Shea Stadium	
Freeport	Freeport Stadium	
Glens Falls	Civic Center	
Hempstead	Hofstra Stadium	
Hempstead	Hofstra College Gym	
Jericho	Hamlet Tennis Center	
New York	Madison Square Garden (old)	
New York	Madison Square Garden (new)	
New York	Polo Grounds	
New York	Yankee Stadium	
Rochester	War Memorial Auditorium	
Schenectady	Alexander Field	
Troy	RPI Field House	
Uniondale	Nassau Coliseum	
West Point	Army Field House	
West Point	Tate Rink	

Stadiums and Arenas Visited

Location	Current Name	Previous Name(s)
North Carolina		
Greensboro	Greensboro Coliseum	
Ohio		
Cincinnati	Crosley Field	
Cincinnati	Cinergy Field	Riverfront Stadium
Cincinnati	Riverfront Coliseum	
Richfield	Richfield Coliseum	
Cleveland	Cleveland Stadium	Municipal Stadium
Ontario		
Barrie	Barrie Arena	
Oshawa	Oshawa Civic Center	
Ottawa	Ottawa Civic Center	
Toronto	Exhibition Stadium	
Toronto	Maple Leaf Gardens	
Toronto	Sky Dome	
Pennsylvania		
Hershey	Hersheypark Arena	
Philadelphia	Civic Center	Convention Hall
Philadelphia	Connie Mack Stadium	Shibe Park
Philadelphia	Core States Spectrum	The Spectrum
Philadelphia	Franklin Field	
Philadelphia	The Palestra	
Philadelphia	Veterans Stadium	
Pittsburgh	Civic Arena	
Pittsburgh	Three Rivers Stadium	
Quebec		
Montreal	Jerry Park	
Montreal	Montreal Forum	
Montreal	Olympic Stadium	
Quebec	Le Colisee	

Stadiums and Arenas Visited

Location	Current Name	Previous Name(s)
Rhode Island		
Providence	Providence Civic Center	
Tennessee		
Memphis	The Pyramid	
Texas		
Dallas	Arlington Stadium	
Dallas	Reunion Arena	
Dallas	Texas Stadium	
Fort Worth	Will Rogers Coliseum	
Houston	Astrodome	
Vermont		
Middlebury	Porter Field	
Washington		
Seattle	Kingdome	
Seattle	Key Arena	Seatttle Center Coliseum
Wisconsin		
Milwaukee	Bradley Center	
Milwaukee	County Stadium	

To order on your credit card call toll free
U.S./Canada 1-800-882-3273 or
ORDER WITH THIS COUPON

VANTAGE PRESS, INC.
516 West 34th Street, N.Y., N.Y. 10001

Please send me _____ copies of

50 YEARS AT THE GAME
A Sports Traveler's Journey
At $14.95/copy plus $2.50 postage & handling
(Please make checks payable in U.S. dollars.)

Name _____

Address _____

City _____ State _____ Zip _____

❑ Check Enclosed   ❑ Visa   ` ❑ MasterCard
❑ Amer. Ex.   ❑ Optima   Exp. Date _____

Card # _____

Signature _____

N.Y. State residents please add sales tax.